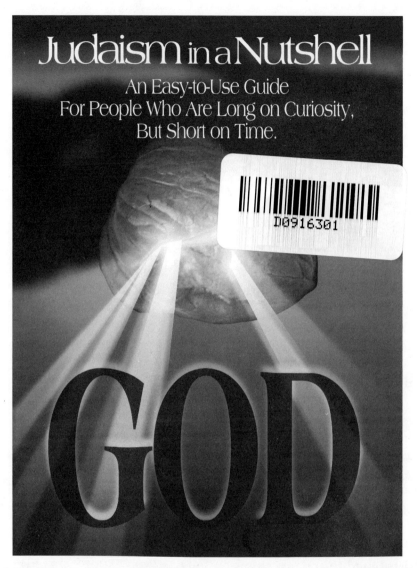

Judaism in a Nutshell

An Easy-to-Use Guide
For People Who Are Long on Curiosity,
But Short on Time.

GOD

"*A delightful and creative work that helps those of us struggling with the concept of God. This book allows us to get in touch with the unfathomable.*"
Dr. Sonya Friedman, Psychologist, Author and Host of CNN's *Sonya Live*

"*Reader beware: this is not the God you met in Hebrew school! It is no mean feat to render complex concepts in simple, conversational language. Judaism has been enriched from this profoundly generous book.*"
Rabbi Avi Weinstein, Director of Hillel's Joseph Meyerhoff Center for Jewish Living

"*A brilliant book that will just astound you. Apisdorf takes complex concepts and makes them not only easy to understand but fun to read.*"
Bob Burg, Author, *Winning Without Intimidation*

Judaism in a Nutshell: God
by Shimon Apisdorf

Copyright © 2001

Leviathan Press
17 Warren Road Suite 18
Pikesville, Maryland 21208
(410) 653-0300
www.leviathanpress.com

ISBN 1-881927-21-0

Printed in the United States of America
First edition
Cover design by Staiman Design
Page layout by Fisherman Sam and Herzog Design
Technical consultants: E.R./D.L./Y.B.Z./B.C.
Editorial services by Sharon Goldinger/PeopleSpeak

Distributed to the trade by NBN (800) 462-6420
Distributed to Judaica stores by Judaica Press (800) 972-6201

All books from Leviathan Press are available at bulk order discounts for educational, promotional and fund raising purposes. For information call (800) 538-4284.
Titles include:
Rosh Hashanah Yom Kippur Survival Kit
Chanukah: Eight Nights of Light, Eight Gifts for the Soul
One Hour Purim Primer   Remember My Soul
Passover Survival Kit   Survival Kit Family Haggadah
Bible for the Clueless but Curious   Death of Cupid
Missiles, Masks, and Miracles   Judaism in a Nutshell: Holidays

ACKNOWLEDGEMENTS

Rabbi Michel and Rebbetzin Feige Twerski, Michael Monson, Rabbi Menachem Goldberger, Michael Schatel, Bill Hackney, Yigal Segal, Tobey Herzog. Sharon Auerbach, Brian Appelstein, Tali Katz, Aryeh Mezei, Nachum Shapiro, Rabbi Avraham Goldhar, Bruce Green, Stella Rae, and special thanks to Mr. David Baum.

SPECIAL THANKS

My parents, David and Bernice Apisdorf. You're the greatest.

Mr. and Mrs. Robert and Charlotte Rothenburg. May you be blessed with years of health and *nachas*.

Esther Rivka, Ditzah Leah, Yitzchak Ben Zion, and Baruch Chananya. This year in Jerusalem.

Miriam. A heroine of the spirit. It all happens thanks to you.

Hakadosh Baruch Hu, source of all blessing.

This book is dedicated in memory of
Rabbi Shmuel Yaacov Weinberg zt"l

*With the passing of Yaacov, the eyes and
the hearts of Israel were closed.*

table of *contents*

introduction

If all of Judaism could be summarized in one word, that word would be God.

When people around the world were worshiping thunder and wind, the Jews had but one word to say—God. When people were lionizing the Spartan and the gladiator, the Jews had but one word to say—God. When life and history called on people to revel in their basest nature, to dehumanize themselves and others, the Jews had but one word to say—God. And when, in every age, people searched for meaning, sanctity, and spirituality, the Jews had but one word to say—God.

> "They were the first people to arrive at an abstract notion of God and to forbid his representation by images. No people has produced a greater historical impact from such comparatively insignificant origins and resources..."
>
> J.M. Roberts, *History of the World* [i]

> "Above all, the Jews taught us how to rationalize the unknown. The result was monotheism and the three great religions that profess it. It is almost beyond our capacity to imagine how the world would have fared if they had never emerged."
>
> Paul Johnson, *A History of the Jews* [ii]

The United States of America was founded on the principle of separation of church and state and at the same time proclaims "...men are created equal, that they are endowed by their Creator with certain unalienable Rights..." While it is tempting to see America as the leader in a worldwide embrace of secularism, the fact is the Gallup Organization has found that 96 percent of Americans believe in God and 90 percent pray regularly. Beyond the borders of America are another three and a half billion Christians and Moslems who worship the God that the Jews introduced to humankind.

It is safe to say that more people believe in God than watch the Super Bowl, MTV, or the World Cup. More people believe in

God than communism, existentialism, and vegetarianism combined, and more people are invested in God than in the stock market. The difference is that people know what the words World Cup, communism, and stock market mean. The word God, however, is another story altogether. People tend to have a wide range of beliefs and ideas when it comes to God.

The goal of this book is to present a coherent picture of the classical Jewish understanding of God and His relationship to creation, to humankind, and to the Jewish people. Historically, it is the Jews who were the first to conceptualize the One transcendent God for humankind. To the Jews, however, God is far more than a concept. God and spirituality are, and always have been, at the heart of the Jewish life experience. Matters of the soul and spirituality are at least as intrinsic to Jewish living as are concerns about cholesterol levels and retirement plans.

The sources upon which this book are based include Maimonides's *Thirteen Principles* and *Mishne Torah*, *Nefesh Hachaim* by Rabbi Chaim of Volozhin, the writings of Rabbi Eliyahu E. Dessler, *Derech Hashem* by Rabbi Moshe Chaim Luzzato, and *Fundamentals and Faith* by Rabbi Yaacov Weinberg.

It would be impossible, however, to even approach a sound understanding of God without having access to great teachers. It is impossible for me to overstate the impact of two master teachers whom I have been privileged to learn from: Rabbi Noah Weinberg, dean of Aish HaTorah Jerusalem, and the late Rabbi Shmuel Yaacov Weinberg, dean of the Ner Israel Rabbinical College. Not a day goes by that my understanding of and relationship to God aren't profoundly informed by their teachings. My dear friend Rabbi Asher Resnick has contributed immeasurably to my understanding of the ideas presented in this book. I have tried to accurately present the classical Jewish understanding of God. I only hope that, despite my failings, this book offers a meaningful introduction to God.

Ohr chadash al tzion ta'ir;
V'nizkeh kulanu m'hayra l'oroh.
Baruch atah Hashem, yotzer ha'meorot.

it all begins with

God

1

God Is Unfathomable

It is impossible to define God in any meaningful way. Here's why:

We live in a world of startling and astonishing beauty. A wondrous three-D world of height, length and width. Far more than mathematical concepts, these three dimensions are the bricks and mortar of our environment and are inseparably linked to the existence of physical matter as well as space. Now suppose for a moment that we lived in a slightly less awesome two-D world, a world lacking height, for instance. I'd like you to actually try that as an imaginative exercise: Before reading any further, take a couple of minutes, close your eyes, and try to imagine what your world would look like if it were heightless.

{ space for imagining }

{ more space for imagining }

As my kids would say, "That's totally weird." In the heightless world you imagined, everything was probably very flat—flat people, flat tugboats, even flat elephants. You see, a heightless world is one in which there is no height *at all*, not even a seventy-second of an inch. So in a truly two-dimensional heightless world, while objects could be long and wide, they would have to be so flat that a grain of sand would tower over them, and in truth, they'd be even flatter than that. Now do you know what my kids mean when they say, "That's totally weird"?

I'd like to take this exercise a little further. Imagine that you are now removing the dimension of length from your already heightless world. Good. Next try removing depth. Good. Now try to imagine squeezing an elephant into your dimensionless world. Tricky, isn't it? But wait, it gets even weirder.

You are now imagining a nondimensional world, a world that can't possibly contain anything, because by removing all three dimensions you have not only eliminated all matter, you have also eliminated space. So even if you imagined a super-squished elephant, there would be nowhere to put him. Believe it or not, there is still something else you can remove from this world. I know that it looks awfully empty already, but I want you to get rid of just one more little thing. I want you to get rid of time itself. This means that even if you could find your elephant, you couldn't do anything with him because *doing* always takes time (even a trillionth of a second), and there is no time.

You are now getting a sense of why the Jewish understanding of God is that He is unfathomable and why discussing what He *is* in any meaningful way is absurd. You see, God created the dimensions of height, length, and width; He created space and matter, and He also created time. This means that whatever God *is*—His being—the nature of His existence, is one that is totally independent of time, space, dimension, and matter. If He created the three-dimensional world of space and matter, then His existence is not confined or defined by these creations because His existence predates theirs. The same is true with time. He existed before time existed and therefore His existence is in no way bound or affected by time.

God is absolutely independent of everything that comprises the reality in which we live. We, being stuck as we are in a time-bound, three-dimensional existence, have no way of conceiving of a reality that could exist independent of all these attributes. So, if you had a hard time conceiving of a dimensionless elephant, you will never be able to grasp what God is.

But don't worry, neither can anybody else.

Is There Anything We Know About God?

Is God entirely beyond comprehension?

Yes and no.

First the no: We can't know, conceive of, or speak of what God *is* because we are utterly without the tools and ability to grasp any semblance of what He is. Since our entire existence takes place within a world of time, we can't possibly imagine an existence where there is no time. Likewise with space and matter—we can't even begin to conceive of an existence where there is no space or matter. If we are asked to conceive of a reality that has no space and matter and no time, most likely the only word that we would find to describe this reality would be "nothing." If you remove all of the basic elements of existence, then what you have is *non*-existence—absolute nothingness. But that's not exactly true because even if you delete everything comprising all of existence, God still exists. And He is none the worse for the absence of mere trivialities like matter, space, and time.

All that we know of God is that His being is fully independent of anything that exists in our reality.

And now for the yes: While we can't even begin to know God directly, we can know a little bit *about* Him. The difference between knowing God Himself and knowing something about God is a little like the difference between renting a furnished oceanfront apartment from a friend and renting the same apartment from a reclusive stranger and never dealing with anyone but the real estate agent. Think about it. When you rent from the stranger through an agent, you will encounter a wide variety of items that give you some idea of who the owner is. The style of furniture, the pattern on the dinnerware, the books on the shelves, the art on the walls, the preset stations on the remote control, all of these, and more. From all of these you will be able to know something about the person in whose home you are now living, but you still won't know the person himself. It's similar with God; from the fact that He created all that exists we can discover certain insights *about* Him, though we remain far removed from knowing Who or What He actually *is*.

Five Things We Know *About* God

Always Read the Warning Label

(**CAUTION**: When one begins to speak about God, one is immediately on a slippery slope that can lead to misleading anthropomorphic conclusions. Therefore, it is important to point out that whenever we apply human terms to God—terms like God's "seeing" or "speaking" or "thinking"—this is done only because we have no other terms in which to speak. These terms are meant to give us a sense of an idea or concept, but in actuality God doesn't "see" in the way we think of seeing and He doesn't "speak" in the way we think of speaking. So we use these terms only as metaphors to give us an inkling of a far greater and indescribable reality.)

1) Absolute Being

God's existence is absolute. The notion that God's being is absolute includes the following: He is fully complete in and of Himself. The nature of His completeness is such that He lacks nothing and needs nothing. God also has no restrictions or limitations and, as such, nothing can exist "outside" of Him, because if anything were able to exist in a way that was separate from His existence, then there would be some sort of a dividing line between these two existences. And all dividing lines indicate a boundary or limitation of sorts. God, the absolute being, has no bounds or limitations. Additionally, absolute being means that His existence is unchanging. God never becomes "more" or "less" in any way; He is never different.

Lastly, absolute being means that His existence is self-sufficient. Hang on to your hats for this one: To say that God has always existed and required nothing to initiate His existence, and to further say that He will always exist and needs nothing to maintain His existence is true, though somewhat inaccurate. The inaccuracy has to do with the issue of time. Since God's being exists even when time does not exist, this means that concepts like *always*, *before*, and *after* have no relevance to His being. So it's not that He always existed and always will exist, it's just that He is. Get it?

2) Independent Existence

Imagine:

Close your eyes and imagine that you are standing in a broad, rolling meadow. Fresh spring grass, daisies, and buttercups gently sway in the breeze. A cloudless french blue sky stretches on forever, and a young boy is running through the meadow clutching a string that stretches high up to a kite.

Now open your eyes:

It's time to turn off your imagination and return to wherever you are, which probably isn't the middle of a meadow.

Were that meadow and that boy real, or were they just the stuff of your imagination? The answer is both. On the one hand there *was* some reality to that meadow, so much so that it could actually produce the feeling of being there. At the same time, it *was* just your imagination, and whatever reality it had was completely dependent on you. As long as you were choosing to focus your mind on that little boy in the meadow, his kite would fly; however, the moment you focused elsewhere, he, his kite, and the whole meadow would simply cease to exist. In a sense, this is a description of the relationship of our existence to God's.

Let's consider the nature of our existence as compared to God's. The perspective we will examine is the difference between Creator and creature. Let's start with the creatures, the ones created by God. This includes everything—from quarks to butterflies and from minerals in the soil to stars in distant galaxies, and us.

The status of being a creation includes the following: Creation couldn't have created itself; therefore, it never could have come into being without God. Creation owes its existence to God. But there is more: the nature of creation can be seen in one of two ways. One way is the autopilot model. In this model, God created everything, hit a cosmic Start button, and the whole contraption has been running on its own ever since. The second model is quite different. In this model, the act of creation itself is an everpresent, ongoing reality. This means that creation was not a one-time event, rather that God is creating everything anew at every instant. This is the classical Jewish understanding of creation.

The consequence of an ongoing renewal of creation is that there are two types of existence, one that is wholly independent and one that is utterly dependent. Want to guess which one is the Creator and which is the creature? That's right! God's existence is independent. This means that if everything ceased to exist—us, our breakfast cereal, and the farthest star in the farthest galaxy—their lack of existence would in no way affect God. The being of the Creator is fully complete, self-sufficient, and independent from His creation.

As for us creatures, that's a different story. We are utterly dependent. This means that since God is "creating" every moment again and again, all of reality is continually and absolutely dependent on God's constant renewal of existence. The moment God decides not to hit that cosmic Refresh button, poof, everything ceases to exist.

3) Involved Supervisor

Until this point we have spoken of God as the Creator. We also saw that the nature of creation is such that He constantly sustains creation. This maintenance of creation is a function of the ongoingness of creation. A direct result of God being the Creator and Sustainer of all existence is that He is also a very hands-on supervisor. Think about it: if every moment is in fact a new act of creation, then God is involved, so to speak, with everything that exists at all times. In other words, God isn't like the owner of a football team sitting comfortably in his luxury box watching a team he owns but has little direct impact on in terms of what takes place on the field. Rather, God is the owner, the general manager, the coach, the water boy and a whole lot more all rolled into one. In other words, He is constantly and intimately involved with all that exists in His creation.

4) Oneness

If all of Judaism could be distilled into one statement it would be, "Listen, O' Israel, God our Lord; God is One."

This is often understood as the proclamation of the Jewish belief in monotheism, one God. In fact, it is much more than that. It is a statement about the unity—the oneness—of God's absolute being. It's true that Judaism gave the world the single most revolutionary idea that has ever been articulated; namely, that there is *only* one God and not a myriad of conflicting and competing gods, forces, and powers. However, the oneness of God means even more than that. The oneness of God means that all that exists, all forces and all powers, are an expression of a greater, transcendent Unity that is the source of their existence as well as the source of any power or influence they seem to exert within existence.

5) Giver

One thing we know for sure about creation is that it doesn't exist *for* God. Since God is wholly complete and lacks nothing, it can't be that His act of creation was motivated by a need, because a need implies a lack and He has no lackings. Creation, then, is not for the Creator; rather, it is *for* the creature. So another critical insight we have *about* God is that His ongoing acts of creation are ongoing acts of altruism. The creation and maintenance of all existence is an act motivated, so to speak, only by pure benevolence. God's "relationship," therefore, to His creation is one in which He is the giver par excellence, and we, the creatures, are the receivers of what it is that God has to offer. And what is it that God has to offer? The only thing that truly exists—Himself.

Abraham Meet God, God Meet Abraham

We are now going to take a short detour from our discussion about God to meet the person who was responsible for introducing mankind to the transcendent absolute being Who is One, Who is independent, Who is the Creator, Sustainer, and Supervisor of all existence and Whose relationship to existence is one of pure bestower of ultimate good. And just who is this person? His name is Abraham.

Freedom Is Bad

For a moment, let's pretend that the bedrock assumption of our society and the central notion that shapes our values, ethics, culture, personal interaction and social policies is the belief that all men are *not* created equal, and that human freedom is, in almost all instances, bad.

Hard to imagine, isn't it?

But what if it were so, and what if this had been the core assumption that shaped world civilization for the last thousand years? And now, imagine that you were born into such a world—a world that for all intents and purposes had always believed that all people are not created equal. Do you honestly believe that it would ever cross your mind that all people might actually be equal, that human liberty and freedom were noble ideals, and that all people possessed an inherent right to make life's most basic and pivotal choices? What if ideas such as these had never been expressed in all of human history? Not only had they never been debated, written about, or spoken of, *ever*, but no one had even entertained the absurd idea that all human beings were equal and that freedom was good.

This Was the World of Abraham

The world into which Abraham was born looked out at the vast panorama of all it saw and experienced and concluded that there were only two types of beings—puppets and puppeteers. The puppets came in many forms. All animals and plants were puppets, and so were rain drops, cities, and people. Pulling the strings of every puppet was a puppeteer; these were the gods. The world in which Abraham was raised—the world in which he learned to speak, formulate thoughts, and interact with people—was a world of cosmic manipulation. That's what everyone assumed and thought, that's what everyone said, and it was on this basis that life was built.

So what do the lives of human puppets look like? How do they view themselves and how do they relate to life and the world around them? The puppet people of the ancient world saw themselves and everything else as "only an imperfect copy of the primal cosmos."[1] Indeed, "Since man was created by the gods to serve them, and he and his civilization were regarded as imperfect copies of heavenly prototypes, there was little feeling of joy or optimism."[2] The picture that history paints for us of life at the time of Abraham is one that said since people were mere puppets on the strings of the gods, life was reduced to worship of and sacrifice to the gods in the hope that by being nice to the puppeteer, he/she/it would be nice to you too. Life had no ultimate meaning or purpose, and there were no such concepts as personal freedom or aspirations since the strings that tied one to the gods could never be severed. No human being could ever have a higher calling, and there were no great values worth devoting one's life to, much less worth dying for.

> *"The Sumerians,* [the people who populated the ancient Mesopotamian world into which Abraham would eventually be born] *not surprisingly, saw themselves as a people created to labor for the gods. These gods demanded propitiation and submission in elaborate ritual. In return for this and living a good life they would grant prosperity and length of days, but no more.*
>
> J.M. Roberts, *History of the World* [3]

At the dawn of civilization, the limits of human aspiration, and the best that one could hope for, was a long and prosperous life. In the end, life was nothing more than a grueling effort to eke out the minimal necessities and comforts of life, all the while hoping that the gods, despite their mercurial whims, would play along. It is no wonder, then, that anything and everything could be an object of worship and that people withheld nothing—even their own children—from the voracious sacrificial appetite of the gods. *This* was the world of Abraham.

Abraham Came to a Different Conclusion

> *"There is hardly an animal in nature, from the Egyptian scarab to the Hindu elephant, that has not somewhere been worshiped as a god."*
>
> Will Durant, *Our Oriental Heritage* [4]

Somehow, Abraham came to a different conclusion. Where everyone saw diversity, Abraham saw unity. Where everyone saw countless phenomena with countless causes, Abraham saw one creation and one Creator. Where everyone saw a panoply of self-serving and self-indulgent cosmic puppeteers, Abraham saw a flawless being who was pure kindness, who only gave and gave the greatest good.

To Abraham nothing could be clearer than the fact that everyone else was dead wrong. Abraham's conception of life was one that envisioned higher aspirations; to Abraham, life had meaning and purpose. To Abraham, there was something deeply noble to strive for in life. For Abraham, there was something to accomplish, something to strive for, somewhere to go in life.

Abraham didn't just come to a different conclusion from everyone else about God. Rather, he was the only person whose thinking concluded with God. The difference between Abraham and every other person on earth was something like the difference between a toddler who trembles at the sound of thunder and is convinced that his mother's skirt can protect him, and an adult who is awestruck by the grandeur of creation.

Abraham Says Adios

Abraham was so sure he was right that the Creator Himself confirmed his convictions.

> *"And God said to Abraham 'Lech Lecha, Go for yourself [not for Me] and leave your land, the community of your birth, and your father's home.'"*

> Genesis 12:1

"If we had lived in the second millennium BC, the millennium of Abraham, and could have canvassed all the nations of the earth, what would they have said of Abraham's journey? In most of Africa and Europe, where prehistoric animism was the norm and artists were still carving and painting on stone the heavenly symbols of the Great Wheel of Life and Death, they would have laughed at Abraham's madness and pointed to the heavens, where the life of earth had been plotted from all eternity ... a man

cannot escape his fate. The Egyptians would have shaken their heads in disbelief. The early Greeks might have told Abraham the story of Prometheus ... Do not overreach, they would advise; come to resignation. In India, he would be told that time is black, irrational and merciless. Do not set yourself the task of accomplishing something in time, which is only the dominion of suffering. In China, the now anonymous sages whose thoughts would eventually influence the I Ching would caution that there is no purpose in journeys or in any kind of earthly striving ... On every continent, in every society, Abraham would have been given the same advice that wise men as diverse as Heraclitus, Lao-Tsu and Siddhartha would one day give their followers: do not journey but sit; compose yourself by the river of life, meditate on its ceaseless and meaningless flow."

Thomas Cahill, *The Gifts of the Jews* [5]

But somehow, some way, Abraham ignored the collective wisdom of *the entire world*. Not only did Abraham's thinking lead him to God, but the conviction of his conclusion led him to strike out in a direction radically different from any other that had ever been traveled. When God said, "Go," Abraham responded with a small step that was truly a giant leap for mankind.

"And Abraham went, just as God had told him ..."

Genesis 12:4

Thus began the relationship between Creator and creature that is inherent in the existence of God the absolute being—Creator, Sustainer, and altruistic and benevolent Supervisor of all creation.

enough with God, what about *Us?*

2

God and Hedonism

Eat, drink, and be merry—the world was created for you.

It seems that the Jewish understanding of God can't help but lead to a hedonistic understanding of life. After all, if creation doesn't exist *for* God, per se, and if we can't do anything for God—because He is complete and has no needs—then it follows that creation must be *for* us and everything we do must also be for us.

Some universities have great academic reputations, some are known for fostering social consciousness, and others are just plain party schools. If everything is ultimately *for* us, doesn't this sound like life is one big party? Consider the following statement of our sages some 2,000 years ago:

> *"Why was the first human being created as a lone individual? [Certainly God could have begun with a family, a village or a whole country had He wanted to.] The reason is that every human being should be able to say to him- or herself—'the world was created for me.'"*

Talmud, Sanhedrin 4b

In other words: Eat, drink, and be merry—the world was created for you!

So What's the Catch?

I'm sure you already suspect that there is some sort of catch to this life-is-just-one-big-party shtick, so I may as well level with you: Life is not one big party—it's the ultimate party!

Think about it. When God does something, He doesn't mess around. (After all, He is God.) He didn't just create any old universe; He created one in which every detail is so strikingly complex and beautiful that one is equally awestruck by something as "simple" as a tulip, as complex as the human eye, or as vast as the Milky Way. The same is true when we say that creation is for us.

If creation is *for* us, what this implies is that existence is for our ultimate benefit; in other words, existence is good for us. However, when Judaism asserts that existence—that life itself—is good for us, we mean this in a different sense from when we say broccoli is good for us. What we mean is that the entire purpose of our existence is that we be the beneficiaries of the greatest good possible. God created us so that we could enjoy being able to receive and partake of the greatest good possible. The key words in all of this are "enjoy" and "good." And just what is this greatest good that we were created to enjoy? It's the Creator Himself.

So there's the catch. The purpose of our existence is to enjoy the experience of God Himself. After all, wouldn't everyone agree that if you could have an experience of God that this would be *the* experience next to which all else would pale?

Do You Want *Your* Children to Attend a Party School?

If you are a parent who cringes at the thought of your child attending a great party school, is this evidence that you have become a rusty old kill-joy? Certainly not. More likely what it means is that you want what is best for your child.

Party schools may be a lot of fun, but they aren't necessarily the best or even the most enjoyable place for people. Of course you want your daughter to have a good time and enjoy her college days. At the same time, you also want her to have an experience that is academically challenging and that helps prepare her to achieve her greater goals in life.

God is the same way (so to speak). He doesn't want us to settle for second best.

> *"When a person leaves this world, she will be asked all sorts of questions about what she did with her life. For instance, if someone had the opportunity to taste an exotic fruit and didn't, she will be asked, 'Why didn't you try the fruit?'"*
>
> Jerusalem Talmud

This statement of our sages highlights the idea that the reason creation exists is for our benefit and enjoyment. Without a doubt, God created the stunning array of fruits He did for us to enjoy, and it's good for us to enjoy God's fruit. But gorgeous, fragrant, juicy, delicious fruits are just the beginning. There's much more where they came from.

Feel the Tug?

Have you ever sat under a quiet starlit sky and asked yourself, "What's it all about?" There is a part of us that is restless, that longs to feel connected to something more in life. It's not that we feel our lives, our jobs, or our relationships are empty; it's just that we sense there is something infinitely deeper—greater—that transcends everything else. We grope for the right words to express our yearning, yet they always seem so inadequate.

If you think back to what we know about God, you will discover the source of this agitation. It's part of the fabric of our being. Remember the part about God's absolute being and His existence being wholly independent while ours is utterly dependent? Remember the part about how our existence is being re-created at each and every moment? Well, let's think about that a little more.

What kind of existence do we really possess if there is nothing we can do to either maintain or sustain it, and it never lasts for more than the blink of an eye? How real is an existence that is utterly helpless, and vanishes the instant after it comes into being?

This is the source of our longing. Deep down, we sense that our lives are desperately fleeting, yet at the same time, we ache for actual, permanent existence. When we long for something "more," it's a longing for something more than ourselves. We are longing for actual being, not ephemeral being. We are longing for God.

Coke Is It

So we were created to enjoy peaches, watermelon, and kiwi and we can't help but long for God. Is that it?

> "So Jacob left Beersheva and headed to Charan. He arrived at a certain place and spent the night there, and he dreamt. And in the dream was a ladder that stood firmly on the earth, while its top reached to the heavens."
>
> Genesis 28:10-12

The ladder that Jacob saw in his dream is an image of life itself.

The experience of life is a five-tiered progression that begins with kiwi and extends to God Himself. It's kind of like the different seats at the ballpark, and it looks like this:

I. Standing Room Only

This area of the stadium doesn't even have seats. This is a small section where people actually pay to stand and watch the game because all the tickets for real seats have been sold out. But at least they are in the ballpark and not at home in front of their televisions. At least here people get to hear the crack of the bat (if their hearing is really good), see the action (if their vision is good), and munch on authentic ballpark franks.

In terms of life, this is your basic realm of physical pleasures. Pleasures like a good massage, a delicious meal, or sitting at the beach and sipping an ice cold Coca-Cola. Sometimes it feels like these pleasures really are the apex of what life has to offer, but we know there is more.

So if Coke *isn't* really "it," if it's not "what you've been looking for," then what is?

II. Reserved Seats

Don't be fooled by the word "reserved," these seats can be so high up you are practically on the roof of the stadium. (I know. It's usually where my kids and I sit). But not only are you in the stadium and not only do you have a seat of your own, the peanut man will actually come by so you can buy a snack without ever leaving your seat—unlike the guy in standing room who risks losing his spot if he ventures out to the Coke stand.

In terms of life, sitting in these seats is like being in the realm of beauty and love. To appreciate beauty in art, in nature, in another human being—this is the beginning of love. Beauty and love are good and wonderful and enormously pleasurable. A cold Coke pales in comparison.

III. Box Seats

Now we're talking. First of all, there is an usher who greets you as you enter this section, shows you to your seat, and wipes it off before you sit down. Then there is the game; you are so close to the field that you not only see the action, you can feel it. *These* are great seats.

In terms of life, these seats are like being in the realm of doing the right thing. For a noble cause, for the sake of justice and goodness, there is little that people won't sacrifice—even love. For the right cause, people are willing to offer their very lives. To do what's right, to live with integrity, and to be a genuinely good person is a profoundly deep pleasure.

IV. Terrace Level Seats

When I was a kid, these seats didn't even exist. The terrace level is a semi-private section of the stadium where only people with the right tickets can enter. Once inside, you feel like you are not only at a game, you're also at a club. There may be waitresses walking around with hors d'oeuvres, there are bars with comfortable chairs to relax in if the game gets a bit slow, and of course the seats are great.

In terms of life, this is the realm of creativity and power. This is where you not only appreciate art, you create it. You not only strive to do what's right, you help build a community or a world that is a better place for mankind. You make a difference, a meaningful difference.

V. Private Luxury Seats

These seats are actually private suites. They have a mini-kitchen with a wet bar, you decorate them as you would your summer home and you can either relax on the couch and watch the game or go out on a porch that features seats that practically hang right over the field. These are no longer seats at the ball park; this is heaven.

In terms of life, this is love of God. Love is the feeling of greatest closeness and deepest intimacy. To love God is to be deeply connected to Him. And, in being connected to God, we shed our ephemeral existence and become part of ultimate, absolute, and actual existence. Through the reality of His being, we too achieve actuality of our being.

In the end it is God, and us, that are the real thing—not Coke.

In the Image of God: What's *That* Supposed to Mean?

Body and Soul

Remember the time when you knew what the right thing to do was but you didn't *feel* like doing it? Like the time when your wife was exhausted and asked you to make dinner, help the kids with their homework, take care of putting them to bed and then do a little grocery shopping? Remember how desperately you wanted to graciously shower her with love and gladly pitch in, while at the same time you felt torn because the final episode of your all-time favorite TV show was on that night? Or what about the time when you had a test to study for but your friends had an extra ticket to a sold out concert you were dying to attend? Or when your doctor told you that your "bad" cholesterol was way too high and you had reservations the next night at your favorite steak house?

Sound familiar? This is the soul and the body.

"And God created the human in His image, in the image of God He created him, both male and female did He create them."

Genesis 1:27

"And God formed the human from the dust of the earth and He breathed into his nostrils the soul of life."

Genesis 2:7

Human beings are at once fundamentally earthy beings as well as intrinsically spiritual. The differences between human beings and angels all stem from one basic distinction; people have bodies and angels don't. Likewise, the difference between human beings and animals goes far beyond the opposable thumb, intelligence, or the ability to think abstractly; the seminal distinction is that people have souls and animals don't.

The Hebrew word for soul, *neshama*, also means "breath." When God "breathed" into the nostrils of man, this means that God joined a soul to the body He had already formed. It is the fusion of these disparate elements, body and soul, that forms the human being. It is also the fusion of body and soul into one holistic being that gives rise to the tension we alluded to earlier.

The Freedom to Choose

Remember that tension between wanting to do what's right while feeling like doing something altogether different? Well, you can find comfort in knowing that you're not the only one who struggles in that way. We all do—constantly. The tension between what we *want* to do and what we *feel* like doing is as intrinsic to our being as our bodies and our souls. The reason is that this tension is actually rooted in the body and the soul. The soul wants to do what's right and meaningful and good; the soul wants to reach outward to others and upward to God. The body would rather have a snack, take a nap, and think about being good tomorrow. So what do we do? The choice is ours, and therein lies the meaning of our being "in the image of God."

We have discussed how God has no limitations and is not subject to constraints of any kind. In this sense, God is completely free. The same is true with us. When it comes to the tension between the disparate elements of our being, we are free to choose as we like. We may choose to do what we want to do or we may choose to do what we feel like doing, but in either case, the choice is ours. This is what being in the image of God means; it means that at the moment of truth when we confront the tension between body and soul, physical and spiritual, we have the fullest freedom to choose.

You, the Indeterminate Creator

Our being in the image of God extends even further. It works like this:

God created us, and so do we.

Who we are, our race, gender, personality, and physical make-up, as well as the time, place, and circumstance of our lives—all of these things—are out of our control. The issue is, what do we *do* with this great package of self that has been left at our doorstep? More directly, from the raw material of our lives, what sort of life do we create?

"Let us make man."

Genesis 1:26

"God therefore addressed this newly fashioned lump of clay which was to be man, and said, 'Let us make man.' You and I together will make man. I will give you the capacities and the potential and I will assist you in the process, but the work must ultimately be your own."

Dr. Abraham J. Twerski, *Let Us Make Man* [6]

It's true that God created us and the world we live in, but in a sense He didn't complete the job. The process of completion is left up to us—His "partners in creation." He gave us everything we need to create a masterpiece, and then He allows us the latitude to give form and shape, texture and color to the final work of art.

This self-creating perspective asks us to view ourselves as active, participatory agents of change, growth, and transformation. It suggests a degree of human potential that borders on the divine.

Free will, then, is the mighty locus of potential that is the ultimate determinate not of who we are but of what we become. The same is true for mankind. Whether the world becomes a masterpiece or a wasteland, the choice is ours.

Nature versus Nurture versus Free Will

No one reading this book hasn't heard of the terms "survival of the fittest" and "behavior modification." That we are either essentially biological creatures whose behavior is predetermined by evolutionary imprints on our genes or that we are clean slates whose behavior is the inescapable result of the particular social factors and experiences to which we have been exposed are notions that have become fundamental to how we view ourselves and the world around us. Consider the following:

> *"Human emotional responses and the more general ethical practices based on them have been programmed to a substantial degree by natural selection over thousands of generations."*
>
> Edward O. Wilson, *On Human Nature* (Pulitzer Prize winner) [7]

And consider this idea from J.B. Watson, the founder of behavioral psychology, who set a course followed by Skinner and others:

> *"Give me a dozen healthy infants, well-formed, and my own specified world to bring them up in and I'll guarantee to take any one at random and train him to become any kind of specialist I might select—doctor, lawyer, artist, merchant-chief, and yes even beggar-man and thief, regardless of his talents, penchants, abilities, vocations, and race of his ancestors."*
>
> J.B. Watson, *Behaviorism* [8]

The issue here goes far beyond the pithy formulation of nature versus nurture. The greater issue is nature versus nurture versus free will. If all behaviors are determined by the biology of nature, then free will goes out the window. Similarly, if it's true that all future behaviors could be predicted if one knew the complete set of all external, social stimuli brought to bear in one's past, then once again, free will would fall by the wayside.

It is important to point out that Judaism looks to biology, chemistry, physics, mathematics, history, anthropology, psychology, and other social and natural sciences as meaningful and beneficial wellsprings of knowledge and insight. The Jewish perspective is that they have much to teach us, just not everything to teach us.

In the end, if Judaism understands anything about God to be true, it's that He is. And if there is anything it understands about people to be true, it's that free will is.

The Buck Stops Here—or—Life Matters

The final factors to understand in the nexus of God's reality and our reality being "in the image of God" are the factors of meaning and responsibility. But first a word from Sartre:

> *"Every existing thing is born without reason, prolongs itself out of weakness and dies by chance."*
>
> Jean-Paul Sartre, *Nausea* [9]

Is it any wonder that the title of Sartre's first great work is Nausea? While it's true that Sartre and others like his Nobel Prize-winning friend, Albert Camus, clearly held that people have absolute free will, at the same time, they felt that since life is, by definition, meaningless (or in the words of Camus "absurd"), it doesn't matter what people do with their free will because all options are equally empty and without meaning.

Jewish understanding comes to a starkly different conclusion; namely, that life is inherently meaningful and valuable, and as such the choices we make and the consequences that flow from them are equally meaningful. In short, life matters.

We will sum these ideas up as follows:

The reality of God and free will is what causes there to be meaningful choices as well as responsibility for one's actions. In practical terms, free will means that it's okay to call some actions good and others bad. More than being okay, it's the right thing to do.

Think about it. If people can't possibly control the way they act, would it not be a grave injustice to ever hold them accountable for their actions? Where there is no free will, praise and punishment are equally absurd. And if what we do or don't do doesn't matter a wit, if it's all nothingness, then again praise and punishment are equally absurd.

In the Jewish way of thinking, there is nothing absurd about existence, life, or the countless choices we are confronted with every day.

Thank God.

Spirituality

3

So What Made God Create the World in the First Place?

This is a question that at one time or another is asked by everyone who thinks about God, and in truth it is a question that can't be fully answered. The reason this question can't be fully answered is that the answer has two components, one that is within our mind's reach and one that isn't. I'll try to explain.

Needs and Motivations

We all have needs in life.

We need food and water to stay alive, we need clothing and shelter, we need to be loved, and we need a sense of meaning and purpose in life. Quite often, it is our needs and their desired fulfillment that are at the root of what motivates us to do what we do. The reason we go grocery shopping, go buffalo hunting, or steal somebody's wallet is that we are hungry. Though very different kinds of actions, they share the same essential motivation; namely, the need to eat. Sometimes it's easy to identify the motivating factors behind our actions and behaviors, while at other times it can be very difficult. Sometimes it's absolutely impossible. With God, it's *always* impossible.

Though God's motivations regarding creation are beyond our ability to comprehend, nonetheless we can discern what the purpose of creation is. A look at archaeology may help clarify the distinction between discerning a purpose and identifying a motivating factor.

Function, Purpose, and Motivation

Picture an archaeologist who has just unearthed an odd-looking object. He examines it carefully, thinks about other items he has dug up in the past, thinks some more about what he already knows about the site he's working on and the people who inhabited it—and scratches his head. He's just not sure what to make of the object he's holding in his hand.

In his quest for understanding, one of his first tasks is to determine the function of the object he has discovered. Was it a container of some sort, a cutting utensil, or perhaps a piece of jewelry? Once he can discern its function—what it seems best suited to do—he then has a very good idea about what its purpose was.

Let's suppose he determines this strange object was a writing instrument. In this case, he would know that the purpose it served was some type of recording, preserving, and communicating of information. Having a sense of both the object's function and purpose, the next question he might reflect on is one of motivation—*what was it that led someone to make this instrument?* Now that's a more difficult question than one of purpose. In a general sense, he will have ideas about what necessitated the invention and construction of this type of item. However, a specific question such as—"Why did someone make *this* particular writing instrument?"—could have numerous possible answers.

While our archaeologist may discover function and purpose, and while he may be able to figure out what role such objects played in this long-gone culture, when looking at a specific object, he is at a loss as to what motivated the craftsman to make that particular one. Perhaps the person who made it did so in order to barter it for something else. Perhaps he was an ancient scribe who had a sacred duty to craft his own writing instrument or perhaps it was a traditional gift that was included in a rite-of-passage ceremony and would be presented to his son when he came of age.

Consider the following archaeological puzzle.

In 1940, some French boys were out having a good time when they wandered into a cave and stumbled upon twelve-thousand-year-old cave paintings. Ask three different scholars and you will get three different hypotheses about what motivated those cave dwellers to paint the walls of their caves the way they did. Were they trying to invoke a spirit to help them in their next hunt? Were they recording some seminal event about their history? Were these paintings an early form of self-expression through art, or were these painters just tired of the old wallpaper? Most likely, we'll never know. The reason we will probably never know for sure what motivated the original painters is that we just know too little about them (what they were like, how they lived, what ideas shaped their consciousness) to be able to say with any great confidence, *this* is the reason they did what they did.

Now let's jump ahead in history a little bit.

Imagine that one day you are sitting by the window of your kitchen and a delivery truck stops in front of your neighbor's house and drops off a large box that has the words "Mongoose Mountain Bike" printed on it in big black letters. Let's think about what you know about the contents of that box and what you don't know. What you know is that there is a bicycle inside. More than that, you know what the purpose of that bicycle is. Its purpose is transportation. What you don't know is what motivated your neighbor to buy this bike in the first place. Did he buy it because his doctor told him it would be a good form of exercise, because his wife is a bicycle enthusiast, or perhaps it's a birthday present for his nephew? On the other hand, he could have paid next to nothing for it at an online auction and plans to sell it and make a little cash. Now let's imagine that this is a neighbor whom you barely know and rarely speak to. Chances are, you may never know for sure why he bought that bike. So where does this leave us?

You know the function of all bicycles, and you do understand the purpose they serve, but as to *this* particular bike, you have no idea what actually motivated your neighbor to purchase it.

This is kind of how it is with God and His creation. We can discern what the purpose of creation is (just like we can discern the purpose of a bicycle or a shovel), but we can't discern the motivation behind creation. This is true for at least two reasons. First of all, since we can't know God and have nothing in common with Him, we can't know what motivates Him. This isn't completely true for those French cave painters or your neighbor. You do seem to have something in common with them; you do know them—at least to some extent—and thus you can sort of put yourself in their place and surmise what possible motivations may lie behind their actions. But God is an altogether different story. He is so utterly different from us that we can't begin to put ourselves in His place in order to get a feel for what might have motivated Him. Second, unlike us, God has no needs. Therefore His "motivation" for creation can't possibly be understood in terms of filling a need.

In the end, while we can know the purpose for which God created us, we can't know *why* He created us. In order to know the why behind an action, you need to either understand the source of the action, the need it fulfills, or preferably both. When it comes to God, since we can't know Him and since He has no needs, we have no way of relating to the question, "Why did God create the universe in the first place?"

Relationship, the Purpose of Creation

When looking at God's creation, and particularly when looking at ourselves, we can deal with the questions of function and purpose, though we can never meaningfully deal with the issue of God's motivation per se.

As we have already discussed, one thing we know for sure about the purpose of creation is that it can't exist *for* God. Since prior to creation God was perfectly complete and lacked nothing, it can't be that He needed to create, because a need implies a lack, and He had, and still has, no lackings whatsoever.

It is for this reason that Judaism has always understood that creation is *for* us. It is we who gain or benefit from the fact of our existence, not God.

> *"The human being was not created for any purpose other than to have the pleasure of God Himself and to savor the delight of His presence; for this is not only the greatest pleasure available but the essence of all true pleasure that can be experienced."*

Rabbi Moshe C. Luzzato, 18th century philosopher and mystic [10]

> *"My being and my heart all but leave me in their longing for You; the deepest part of me yearns, that my lot in life be God: forever. Those who are distant from You become lost, You destroy those who separate themselves from You. And I, the only thing I call good is my closeness to You ..."*

David, 7th century BCE,
scholar, musician, giant slayer, and king of Israel [11]

Creation is for us. It's for our good, and the greatest possible good is God. It's for our pleasure, and the greatest possible pleasure is God. This is how Jews from ancient times until this very day have always understood the purpose of creation, and this is what was implied earlier when we said that God's "relationship" to us is one in which He is the giver par excellence and we, His creations, have the capacity to receive that which God has to offer. And what is it that God has to offer? The only thing that truly exists—Himself.

That creation is *for* us means that we have the potential to achieve closeness to God. This doesn't mean closeness in the sense of proximity, but closeness in the sense that two friends can be "close," and a husband and a wife can share a closeness that defies description and transcends even the greatest physical distance and obstacles.

We call this closeness a relationship.

That creation is for us means that we have the potential to be intimately connected to our Creator—to God—through a relationship.

Function and the Longing for Unity

> *"We inherit our legacy in the sciences and the arts—works of great Discoverers and Creators, the Columbuses, the Leonardos, and Shakespeares. We glory in their discoveries and creations. But we are all seekers."*

Daniel J. Boorstin, Librarian of Congress Emeritus, *The Seekers*[12]

We function as beings who look and long and seek.

More than wanting to understand things, we are driven to understand them. More than looking for meaning in life, we yearn for it. We not only seek answers and meaning, we long for them.

You will recall that the nature of our existence—of all created existence—is that we are re-created at each and every moment. As such, in essence, our existence is at best transitory and even borders on the illusory. Every moment of existence is one over which we have no power and which, in any case, vanishes the instant after it comes to be. Utter tenuousness is the inescapable constant of life.

And so we long. We long for a state of being beyond our own. We long to transcend the flimsiness of our reality, and to somehow become a part of something that will enable us to be *more*.

The *more* that we are seeking can only be God Himself. Everything else, like us, is ephemeral. Nothing other than God has any *more* actuality than we do. But we have more than just a blind longing. Though we may never articulate it, deep down we know what we are longing for. We know what it is we are seeking. In seeking God, we seek what is known in Hebrew as *echad*, the oneness and unity of actual absolute being.

I'd like you to try an exercise now. Make a list of your most meaningful and pleasurable experiences in life.

My life's most meaningful and pleasurable experiences:

1.
2.
3.
4.
5.
6.
7.
8.
9.
10.

Now look at your list and ask yourself "What was the essential ingredient present in those experiences that enabled me to include them on my list?"

As you begin to track down the essence of those experiences, what you will find at the core of most, if not all, of them is *echad*— a oneness, a unity, a harmonious sense of things merging and melding together. Surely some of the following were on your list:

A special friendship: Sharing, caring and connecting in a rare and deep way—*echad*.

Mastering a skill: The awkward gap between yourself and the piano, the golf club or the computer finally narrows to the point of disappearing, until you are finally "at one" with the piano—*echad*.

Skiing:	You are alone with the morning's early light and winding your way down a slope blanketed in virgin snow; you are one with the mountain—*echad*.
Enjoying music:	You close your eyes and not only hear the music, you feel the subtle nuance of every note; something inside begins to soar as you become a part of the music and it becomes a part of you—*echad*.
Love of a spouse:	Where the innermost parts of oneself are shared with another. Where the boundaries between "I" and "We" become permeable—*echad*.
Gaining a new insight:	The joy of "Aha, now I get it." When suddenly all the confusing pieces come together in one logical and beautiful picture—*echad*.
Teamwork:	When everybody is able to see beyond themselves and pull together for a common goal—*echad*.
Beauty:	Where do you see beauty? In art, in nature, in a gentle, caring, giving human being? Do you sense it in all of them?—*echad*.

Science too, it seems, boils down to the search for an elegant, beautiful, and unified understanding of all that exists in the natural world—*echad*.

Consider the following:

> *"Inevitable, simple, congruent with the whole: Those are the hallmarks of a beautiful theory. It is, in fact, this aesthetic yearning for congruity with the whole that has spurred on physicists of the last two centuries to search for a Theory of Everything that could encompass all physical phenomena in the universe and unify the four fundamental forces of nature."*

> Trinh Xuan Thuan, *Chaos and Harmony*[13]

"Still, relying on this intuitive idea that different scientific generalizations explain others, we have a sense of direction in science. There are arrows of scientific explanation that thread through the space of all scientific generalizations. Having discovered many of these arrows, we can now look at the pattern that has emerged and we notice a remarkable thing: perhaps the greatest scientific discovery of all. These arrows seem to converge to a common source! ... There is reason to believe that in elementary particle physics we are learning something about the logical structure of the Universe at a very, very deep level. We have found that the laws, the physical principles, that describe what we learn become simpler and simpler ... What I am saying is that the rules that we have discovered become increasingly coherent and universal ... there is simplicity, a beauty, that we are finding in the rules that govern matter that mirrors something that is built into the logical structure of the Universe at a very deep level."

Steven Weinberg, Nobel Prize-winning physicist[14]

"In our century it was Albert Einstein who most explicitly pursued the goal of a final theory. The last thirty years of Einstein's life were largely devoted to a search for a so-called unified field theory .

"If there were anything we could discover in nature that would give us some special insight into the handiwork of God, it would have to be the final laws of nature. Knowing these laws, we would have in our possession the book of rules that govern stars and stones and everything else. So it is natural that Stephen Hawking [A Brief History of Time] should refer to the laws of nature as 'the mind of God.'"

Steven Weinberg, *Dreams of a Final Theory*[15]

The presence of this elegant unity in life, as in nature, like the faint echoes of the Big Bang, serves as a beacon that guides and draws us to ultimate oneness. At the heart of that which we find to be meaningful and pleasurable, we continually discover oneness—because that *is* the pleasure, the meaning, the *more* we are seeking and so desperately long for.

And so, when we look at ourselves as an archaeologist would look at a curious find, what we are able to discern is that we function, all of us, as seekers of oneness. We seek meaning and pleasure and to be more, and in all the experiences that contain a bit of that which we are seeking, we discover oneness. It is from here that we discover the purpose for which we were created.

Creation, our creation, is for us. For our benefit, our good, and our pleasure. And all of these "arrows" lead to God, Whose being is absolute and Whose absoluteness means *echad*, One.

The Quest for Spirituality

Does the following sound familiar?

"Religion doesn't really speak to me. I'm sure it's very satisfying for people who are into it, but I find spirituality in my *own* way. I like taking long walks in the woods or sitting alone and meditating on the sounds of a small brook. There are times when I am out there in nature and I feel like I'm merging with something infinitely greater than myself; there's this feeling of being at peace with the universe. Sometimes I feel that I'm almost walking together with God Himself.

"I think that kind of experience is available to anyone, and that it can be achieved in many different ways. A friend of mine once invited me to attend an all-night Native American ritual. It was unbelievable; you could just see that these people were connecting with something in a very deep way. I mean what's the difference if you are alone on a mountaintop, listening to beautiful music or deep into Krishna? As long as you are a good person and connecting with God, isn't that what it's all about?"

We are living in a time that has been rightfully dubbed, "the information age." In a relatively short period of time, thanks to the advent of the silicon chip, the personal computer, and the Internet, we have come to relate to the world in a fundamentally different way—not only radically different from how our parents related to it, but different from how we ourselves related to it a mere five or ten years ago. We are only beginning to understand the significance and impact that this new age represents and the various consequences that it promises to bequeath.

At the same time, within the greater context of this new age of information, we have seen another significant shift in consciousness. The shift has been away from religion and, oddly enough, towards spirituality. Consider the following:

> *"George Barna, who has been studying changes in religiosity since 1982, says that baby boomers who began returning to churches in the mid-1980s were disappointed and since 1991 have been in 'massive retreat.' At the same time, growing numbers are seeking spiritual and moral grounding through meditation and Eastern religions, while others are attracted to New Age writings and music."*
>
> David Gergen[16]

> *"At the Spiritual Music Festival in Los Angeles, many in the audience like to call themselves spiritual rather than religious."*
>
> National Public Radio[17]

> *"Disenchanted with formal religion, modern-day spiritual seekers are turning to books as inspirational guideposts on life's journey."*
>
> Pythia Peay[18]

> *"If booksellers and publishers had a dollar for every time someone said, 'I'm spiritual but not religious,' they wouldn't have to worry about their retirements. Today's typical seekers try to find their way to the transcendent*

via a personal, experiential and eclectic path rather than through traditional organized religion. Not surprisingly, their book-buying habits have reflected this shift."

Heidi Schlumpf[19]

It's come to the point that spirituality is used to sell, of all things, food!

"RJR Nabisco launched a new campaign this summer that instead pitches the noshes [SnackWell's] as, literally, soul food. They enjoin snackers (specifically, women thirty-five and up) not to 'fill yourself' but to 'FULfill yourself.' Earlier this year, Campbell's Soup adopted the pitch, 'M'm! m'm! good for the body, good for the soul.'"

James Poniewozik[20]

And finally, it turns out that one of the most popular and influential films of all time is actually about the great spiritual quest:

"I see Star Wars as taking all the issues that religion represents and trying to distill them down to a more modern and easily accessible construct ... I put the Force in the movie in order to try to awaken a certain kind of spirituality in young people—more a belief in God than a belief in any particular religious system."

George Lucas[21]

So the issue is, in the context of this great quest for some kind of spirituality, what role, if any, does God play?

The Sons of Aaron: Is God Antispirituality?

There is a terribly unsettling story in the Torah (the Bible) about two men's quest for spirituality. First, the setting:

The high point of Jewish history occurred when God enabled the entire Jewish nation to be immanently aware of His presence at the time of the giving of the Torah at Mount Sinai. Then, following this pinnacle event, God instructed the nation to build a tabernacle that would serve as a kind of portable Mount Sinai. Throughout their travels in the desert, this tabernacle (and in its later permanent form, the Temple in Jerusalem) would be a vehicle through which the presence of God would be manifest in the midst of the Jewish nation.

The construction of the Tabernacle culminated in an eight-day inauguration ceremony that was led by Moses and his brother, Aaron, the High Priest. On the eighth day this great ceremony reached its climax, and we find the following account of what took place:

> *"And Moses and Aaron went into the tent of Divine meeting; and when they exited and blessed the nation, the awesome presence of God became manifest to the entire nation. And a supernatural fire burst forth as if from God Himself and consumed what had been presented on the altar. And the nation broke out in song and prayed that they always be privileged to experience this state of intense awareness of God's presence among them."*
>
> Leviticus 9:23-24

And just at that moment of national spiritual fulfillment:

> *"The sons of Aaron, Nadav and Avihu, each took his pan and put in it a fire along with the special incense. Then, **though they had not been instructed to do so**, they brought this fire into the Tabernacle. And another supernatural fire burst forth and incinerated both of them, and they died right there before God."*
>
> Leviticus 10:1-2

According to our tradition, Nadav and Avihu were great men who were driven by a deep desire for closeness to God. And what happened to them? At that moment of enormous spiritual inspiration, and sensing an unusual opportunity to achieve a rare depth of spiritual connection to God, they reached for a way to express their longing—and they paid with their lives!

But how could this be? So they innovated a bit, is that so terrible? After all, the only reason they did so was because they wanted to reach for God at a moment that was ripe with intense spirituality. And for this they must die? What about our longing for God, what about the yearning for oneness, what about the purpose of creation being able to achieve closeness to God? Is all of this thrown out the window just because Nadav and Avihu didn't act exactly as had been prescribed? What's the deal—are we supposed to strive for closeness to God or aren't we?

A Thought about Relationships

The surest way to kill a relationship is to relate to a person in terms of who you imagine them to be, who you want them to be, or who you wish they were, instead of in terms of who they actually are.

Think about a woman who doesn't particularly like flowers and who can't stand chocolate. The first time her husband brings her a dozen roses and a box of chocolates she will be touched by his thoughtfulness. If, however, she tells him that she's not all that crazy about flowers and chocolate, and he still continues to bring her roses and bonbons, how will she feel then? At that point, the same gift that had once touched her and brought the two of them closer will now drive the two of them apart. Why? Because what is transpiring is that her husband is relating in an inappropriate manner. He's not responding to who she is but rather to who he wants her to be. In essence he's not focused on her and what brings her pleasure, but on himself and what gives him pleasure. And, as we all know, self-centeredness is the death knell of relationships.

Spirituality as a Relationship

Communication is critical to a marriage. The same is true in a relationship with God. Think about it. If God doesn't inform us about how to achieve oneness with Him, if He doesn't guide us in the relationship, is there any way we can hope to achieve this closeness on our own?

While achieving the pleasure of a close relationship with God is *the* purpose of creation, and while attachment to the ultimate One is what it means that creation is *for* us—for our benefit and pleasure—how can we possibly hope to know how to relate to Him if He doesn't communicate? After all, God is always utterly different from us. And if relating meaningfully to a person is impossible without having an idea of what is appropriate in terms of who that person is, then a relationship with God will certainly be hopelessly handicapped if we aren't informed of what is appropriate and meaningful in terms of "Who" He is.

This is the story of Nadav and Avihu. Rather than responding to God's communication, Nadav and Avihu superimposed their own subjective perspective on the relationship. Though everything felt so "right" to them, and though they thought they were achieving closeness to God, in fact, they created ultimate distance. At that moment of intense national closeness to God, the Jewish people were taught that the bedrock of authentic spirituality, of maintaining a close relationship with God, is God's communication. Without it, at best, we are groping in the dark. At worst, we move far away from that which we long so desperately to be close to.

God's Communication

For human beings to have a chance at actualizing the purpose of their existence, it is essential for God to communicate.

It was all very nice that Abraham came to a realization of God, but if God had not reached out and communicated with Abraham, there was very little he could have done with his knowledge. Without communication and direction from God Himself, Abraham would have been left with nothing other than his own best guess as to how, or even if, he could have any type of relationship with the God of his convictions.

This makes the words we quoted earlier all the more significant.

"And God said to Abraham 'Lech Lecha, Go for yourself and leave your land, the community of your birth, and your father's home."

Genesis 12:1

When Abraham first heard the voice of God, he was hearing far more than the affirmation of his intellectual convictions. He was hearing that there was the possibility of a relationship. In essence, when God spoke and Abraham listened, what took place was the actualization of all the basic ingredients for a relationship between man and his Creator.

God doesn't communicate with humans because it's lonely up there and He needs someone to talk to. God communicates because He has to. He created human beings with a purpose, with all the great potential inherent in free will, and in order for them to understand how to actualize this potential, they need a little help from God.

The journey from base camp to the peak of Everest is hard enough even *with* a map; without one it is almost inconceivable. The gap between understanding our purpose and the journey to actualization is far greater than that between the dream of the summit and finally planting a flag at the top of the world. So, in order to put the achievement of our purpose within our reach, in order to make the attainment of closeness and attachment to Him possible, God communicates. His communication is a map, a spiritual map clothed in parchment, like a soul clothed by the body. Does a map make the journey easy? Certainly not. The journey is long and challenging and fraught with dangers, but at the end lies a discovery beyond any we can ever imagine. A relationship with God Himself.

a brief history of

God *(and man)*

4

God the Author

God is the best-selling author of all time.

His book is called the Torah, the Bible, and its influence eclipses that of any other book of ethics, spiritual guidance, fiction, self-help, jurisprudence or history ever written.

> *"The Jews started it all—and by 'it' I mean so many of the things we care about, the underlying values that make all of us, Jew and Gentile, believer and atheist, tick. Without the Jews, we would see the world through different eyes, hear with different ears, even feel with different feelings ... we would think with a different mind, interpret all our experience differently, draw different conclusions from the things that befall us. And we would set a different course for our lives."*
>
> Thomas Cahill, *The Gifts Of The Jews* [22]

> *"Before clocks were invented, frustration had a different shape. The past was a part of the present; individuals*

lived surrounded, in their imagination, by their ancestors and their mythical heroes, who seemed as alive as themselves...But then the Jews invented a new idea of time, which has been adopted by all modern societies: they separated the past clearly from the present. Having made a contract with God, they looked forward to its implementation in the future, not in heaven, but in this world. They were the first to imagine a time when justice would be established, when the deserts would become fertile [this was] the beginning of a new tradition of dreaming about the future."

Theodore Zeldin, *An Intimate History of Humanity* [23]

"For many people during many centuries, mankind's history before the coming of Christianity was the history of the Jews and what they recounted of the history of others. Both were written down in the books called the Old Testament [the Torah], the sacred writings of the Jewish people... They were the first to arrive at an abstract notion of God and to forbid his representation by images. No other people has produced a greater historical impact from such comparatively insignificant origins and resource ..."

J.M. Roberts, *History Of The World* [24]

So God is a best-selling author and the people of His book have had a remarkable impact on mankind; the question is, what is God's book all about? And the answer, it seems, is that it depends who you ask. Some find in His book the roots and principles of morality and human ethics, some find poetry and drama, some find the keys to love and faith while others see a great legal code or a map for archeologists with an interest in the ancient Near East. All of these answers are reflective of how different people with different perspectives, backgrounds, and interests relate to the Torah. But what about God? After all, He is the author. What is the Torah from God's perspective?

God the Historian

"The history of mankind is the history of the progress and development of human knowledge. Universal history, at least, which deals not so much with deeds of individuals or even of nations as with the accomplishments and the failures of the race as a whole, is no other than the account of how mankind's knowledge has grown and changed over the ages.

Universal history, thus conceived as the history of knowledge, is not a chronology of every discovery and invention ever made. Many of them—perhaps most—are ultimately of little value. Instead, it is and must be the story, told in the broadest and most general terms, of the significant new knowledge that humanity has acquired at various epochs and added to the growing store."

Charles Van Doren, *A History of Knowledge* [25]

"I have included the story of only a few crucial inventions ... I have not told the story of the shaping of governments, the waging of wars, the rise and fall of empires. I have not chronicled culture, the story of Man the Creator, of architecture, painting, sculpture, music and literature ... My focus remains on mankind's need to know—to know what is out there."

Daniel J. Boorstin, *The Discoverers* [26]

One way of thinking about history is the chronological timeline approach. This is the way most of us are used to imagining history. In this case, history is a long chain of events that when strung together tell us about what human beings did, or how they responded to what happened to them, at various times and places over the millennia. Another way of thinking about history is a more universal one that sees the human story in terms of a few grand endeavors that are the heartbeat of all history. From this perspective, regardless of time or place, events or personalities, all of history is the unfolding expression of a handful of guiding forces.

The Torah is a uniquely multi-layered document. Its layers are at once legal, mystical, psychological, spiritual, and ethical. At one of its layers it is also historical, and its historical frame-of-reference is particularly panoramic—the Torah is the history of the world from God's perspective. In terms of historical events, developments, and personalities—in terms of the way we usually conceive of history—the Torah is an inadequate document riddled with gaps. But that's not the *kind* of history the Torah deals with. Rather, it is history in its most seminal and universal sense. It is the history of man's struggle to come to terms with the reality and implications of his createdness. In truth, throughout all of human history, there is only one story to be told, one story that has ultimate, absolute, and objective value. This is the story about how a created being—a being who like all other creations is utterly dependent, contingent, and ephemeral—the human being, was given the freedom to choose whether or not to confront the deeply unsettling fact of his being created, and how he used that freedom to either delude himself into a false sense of being or to achieve actual being by forging a bond with his Creator.

From Adam, to Abraham, to Moses to Debbie

Adam*

The first human beings, Adam and Eve, weren't born. They were the direct "hands-on" creation of God Himself, and they knew it. Jewish tradition teaches that Adam possessed a degree of awareness and understanding that was astounding. Commensurate

---

* In speaking about the first human beings, Adam and Eve, I will be referring to them collectively as Adam, or Man. This is not meant to slight Eve or any other women who have come since; it's just a simpler way of doing things. Adam, in our context, means the original, prototypical human being. In truth, the nature of the first human beings is a very deep subject that is dealt with at length in the classical texts and is beyond the scope of this book.

with this depth of understanding of himself, God, and his place in creation, Adam had enormous potential. In fact, his combined abilities were so outstanding that when the angels looked at this creation of God's called Adam, they all but mistook him for a deity that was God's co-equal.

> *"When Adam was created the heavenly angels made a mistake and wanted to describe him with the same word they used to "describe" God—kadosh, holy."*
>
> Midrash

God's history of man's struggle to come to terms with the reality and implications of his createdness began with the story of Adam in the Garden of Eden. (In truth it began earlier, with creation itself—the setting for man's epic struggle—but we are going to skip a few pages and get right to the first account of man's living within creation.) Here's the story in a nutshell:

> *"And God took Adam and placed him in the garden of Eden to work it and to preserve it. And God commanded Adam and said, 'You are permitted to eat from all the trees in the garden. However, you are not permitted to eat from the tree of the knowledge of good and evil, because the day you eat from it you will die."*
>
> Genesis 2:15-16

Whether or not you ever read the book or saw the movie, one way or another you know the gist of this story. Despite God's prohibition and warning, Adam went ahead and ate from the one tree he had been told not to. And the results weren't very pretty.

> *"And God said to Adam, 'Because you listened to your wife and went ahead and ate from the tree that I told you not to eat from, the ground will be cursed because of you, and for the rest of your life you will eat of it only through suffering. Thorns and thistles are what it will sprout for you and you will eat grasses from the field. Only by the sweat of your brow will you eat bread. And this is how it will be until you yourself return to the ground because*

you were originally made from the ground—you are dust—and to this dust will you return."

Genesis 3:17-19

As you can see, it wasn't exactly smooth sailing in the Garden of Eden.

God and Adam

Talk about history beginning on a sour note. All this talk about a relationship between us and God, and right off the bat the situation got rather dysfunctional. What happened?

Let's think about the dilemma that Adam faced.

First of all, let's think about Adam and his perception of himself and his place in creation. What we are going to assume is that Adam's awareness included everything we've discussed so far. It included an awareness of God (He did speak to Adam after all), and a profound awareness that God's existence was fully complete and independent while Adam's own existence was totally dependent and contingent. Adam knew that every moment was a new creation, that he had no ability to affect the beginning or end of that creation, and he was therefore acutely aware that his own existence dangled helplessly at the brink of nonexistence.

Second, Adam was aware that creation was *for* him and that the purpose of his existence was to benefit from the pleasure of a relationship with God. Adam knew that the pleasure that was his purpose necessitated, in some way, the attaching of his limited and precarious being to God's ultimate being.

Finally, Adam knew that he had free will. He knew he had almost limitless potential and that he had been given the independence and freedom to do with that potential whatever he chose.

Now let's try and picture the situation, to the extent that we can, from Adam's perspective. Adam thought to himself, I can do and become and create almost anything I want. My abilities and potential are truly vast. At the same time, I am a prisoner. I am constantly dangling on the end of God's string. Each and every moment of my existence is a new creation. I feel like I am some kind of a light bulb. God turns me on, then off, then on again, then off again—and it never stops. If this is freedom, why do I feel so helpless?

And then Adam thought some more and said to himself ... Come on, Adam old boy, you can figure this thing out, why do you think God gave you that head on your shoulders? Okay, so God created me in His image and gave me freedom and independence. But why? Was this some kind of a cruel joke or does He actually want me to be free? Clearly, He wants me to be free, and what's more—I am free. So it's only natural that I experience an occasional bout of angst when I think about the lack of freedom I seem to have, despite my freedom. Bottom line: I want to be free because God created me to be free. *All* I want is to be what I am, free ...

While all of this was going through Adam's mind there was a knock on the garden gate. You guessed it, it was none other than the great big absolute Creator Himself. He had something to discuss with Adam. "You know all those wonderful trees I put in your garden? Go ahead, enjoy them. There's just one—it's called the tree of the knowledge of good and evil—and that one is off limits. You're not allowed to eat from that one." And with that, God excused Himself.

Meanwhile, back inside Adam's head:

... What's He trying to do to me? Here I am, minding my own business, trying to figure out what's bothering me, and how to fulfill the purpose of my existence—and now this! I'm not allowed to eat from that wheat tree over there. (According to tradition the tree of knowledge was a "wheat tree," and what Adam ate more resembled a saltine than an apple.) What in the world is going on ...?

The Problem Is Worse Than You Thought

In addition to everything that Adam was aware of, there was something else that was crystal clear to him that only complicated matters. Adam knew the answer to the following question:

"... If God created me for the purpose of achieving the pleasure of closeness to Him, why didn't He just make us close in the first place?"

The answer that Adam knew was—

"... If God would have just given me ultimate pleasure as a freebie, then I would never have been able to truly enjoy it. Just the opposite, I would feel lessened by the fact that I was given something for nothing. Isn't it true, after all, that we enjoy things far more when we work to achieve them than when they are just handed to us on a silver platter?"

Think of one of those wrinkled dollar bills stuck to the wall of a store with old yellowed pieces of Scotch tape. Now imagine that this store is quite a successful business and that there are two people working behind the counter. One of them is the old man who started the business fifty-five years ago, and the other is his grandson who has only been there for a couple of years. No matter how big a paycheck the grandson may be taking home, he can't possibly get the same sense of pleasure and satisfaction out of opening up the store in the morning and seeing that old dollar bill that his grandfather gets. His grandfather sees much more than a dollar bill hanging on that wall. He sees years of effort, of ups and downs; he sees the first time his son came to the store with him, he sees the success of building something that could provide a comfortable living for his family, and now he sees a third generation coming into the business. What's the difference between the grandfather and the grandson? One worked for everything he has, and the other didn't.

The awareness of this something-for-nothing-just-isn't-as-pleasurable principle only complicated the issue for Adam. Let's listen in again on his thoughts:

... Okay, so not only am I a helplessly contingent being who God created for the purpose of achieving the pleasure of actual being—by being attached to Him—but He wants me to *earn* that pleasure because if I don't earn it I won't be able to fully enjoy it. Then what does He do? He gives me all this unbelievable ability and potential, couples that with free will, gives me this gorgeous garden to live in, and then tells me ... "by the way, no saltines ..." The only conclusion I can come to is that somehow the key to my fulfilling the purpose of my existence lies in God's wanting me to keep away from crackers ...

Adam Was Right

The key to Adam's fulfilling the purpose of his creation (and thereby the purpose of all creation) *did* lie in God's prohibition. And once again, this only heightened Adam's sense of being confronted with a terrible dilemma. Just listen to the poor guy:

"If I listen to what God tells me to do, if I use all my ability and the potential inherent in my freedom to do exactly what God wants me to do instead of doing what *I* might want to do, aren't I really squandering my great potential? I mean, if all God wants is a robot to carry out His wishes in this world, why did He have to create just the opposite? Why did He have to create such a talented and independent guy like me when all He wanted was a robot? However, if I do go ahead and play the part of the submissive robot and do whatever God wants me to do—regardless of what I myself may or may not want—then won't I actually be attaching myself to Him by being His surrogate, so to speak? In other words, if God wants something to happen and He asks me to be the one to make sure it happens, then aren't I in effect becoming an extension of God Himself? Aren't I becoming as attached to God as one could possibly become? In that case, I finally *would* achieve the actual being that I so desperately long for and the pleasure for which God created me. Must be—I shouldn't go anywhere near that tree."

But something was still bothering Adam.

"There's just one problem with all this. It seems that no matter what I choose, I lose. If I choose to listen to God and thereby become attached to Him but become a robot in the process, haven't I destroyed what God wanted to make in the first place—a free and independent human being? In other words, it just doesn't seem right that the price for fulfilling my human potential is the undoing of that potential, namely, the undoing of my freedom. How could it be that in order to achieve my purpose I have to destroy my essence? But if I *don't* listen to God and instead go off and do my own thing, then that too will only lead me away from my purpose because not only will I not be an emissary of God, but I'll be ignoring Him altogether. What I will be doing is saying to God, 'Thanks for this wonderful existence (dependent though it may be) and thanks for the great potential and the freedom to use it, and—so long, I'm off to explore and enjoy the world, and do it *my* way.'"

What's an Adam to Do?

In the end, Adam chose not to listen to God. Not because he was a bad guy but because he mistakenly concluded that he could best fulfill his purpose by *not* listening to God. Adam figured like this—

"Since God created me with this vast potential and since He has placed before me only the minor tasks of tending garden and not eating saltines, it must be that what He really wants of me is to use my freedom to create an even greater mission for myself. In this way, I will become not only an emissary of God, I'll become His partner. I'll be joining with Him in creating the mission that will ultimately lead to the fulfillment of my purpose. So, just this once, I'm going to ignore God, create distance between the two of us, and then, having created this distance, I'll have to *really* use all my ability to actualize the closeness He wants me to achieve. You see, since it will take much more effort to achieve this closeness by starting from further away, I'll actually end up earning more of the pleasure that God created me for in the first place."

So basically Adam thought he could outsmart God, and that was a big mistake.

The problem was Adam didn't realize how much distance would actually be created by a seemingly small departure from God's wishes. In fact, the distance that Adam created was disastrous, not only for himself but for the entire world. Adam ended up so far away from God that from that point forward the rules of the game would be radically altered. Adam became a different Adam and the world became a different world because of Adam's blunder.

Looking back, Adam realized that his original state of being had been perfectly tuned by God to take into account both his free will, his great potential, the need for him to earn his achievements, and God's desire that he make a choice that would result in the greatest possible closeness and pleasure. He also realized that just as when God created the world it was *for* us, so too, when He communicates, this is also for us—for our benefit, for our good, and ultimately for creating the pleasure of our closeness to Him. But there was no going back; the situation had changed, and changed for the worse. It was now the descendants of Adam who would inherit the wreckage he left behind. It was *they* who would now have before them the great task of undoing the damage and ultimately finding a way back to the achievement of God's purpose for creation.

Easier Said Than Done

The damage inflicted on the world in general, and on humankind in particular, was devastating. When God said to Adam, "*... the ground will be cursed because of you and for the rest of your life you will eat of it only through suffering. Thorns and thistles are what it will sprout for you and you will eat grasses from the field. Only by the sweat of your brow will you eat bread: And this is how it will be until you yourself return to the ground because you were originally made from the ground— you are dust—and to this dust will you return,*" God was telling him that the essential nature of man's relationship to the world, and the world's relationship to him, had changed.

Remember when we discussed how man was created in the image of God and we saw the verse that said "*And God formed the human from the dust of the earth and He breathed into his nostrils the soul of life"*? Well, it was that fundamental balance between the body and the soul that Adam had now disturbed.

Prior to his mistake, though he had a body and a soul, Adam had the luxury of not having to be preoccupied with his physicality. His body was there, but its interests and drives and appetites weren't constantly vying for his attention. All that changed. Now Adam would be constantly immersed in his own physicality and with the earthiness of the world he lived in. In a sense, when Adam became distanced from God, his soul became estranged from its source, God. And at the same time that his soul was losing touch with its source, his body was drawing closer to its source, the dust of the earth. It was this distortion of the essential balance of creation that would make it so difficult for future human beings to become and achieve all that God wanted for them.

From the very beginning of creation, God had the highest hopes for human beings, but the great freedom He had afforded them meant that events wouldn't necessarily work out according to plan. But God doesn't give up so easily.

From Adam to Abraham

From the time of Adam's blunder until the appearance of Abraham on the stage of world history, only three significant events took place. Cain and Abel had a fight and Abel lost. A deluge of Biblical proportions wiped out everyone except for a guy named Noah and his family, and an enormously ambitious construction project known as the Tower of Babel ended in bankruptcy.

Of course, a lot more happened in the nineteen hundred years that passed between the time of Adam and the life of Abraham, but in terms of the overarching meaning of human history, those three events were about it. Here's why.

After Adam messed things up, God decided to stand back (actually Adam had shoved Him aside), take a more laissez-faire approach to matters, and wait for people to rise to the challenge of undoing the damage of Adam. Unfortunately, while God was waiting patiently, there was little effort made in the right direction. In fact, most of what was taking place made matters even worse, and people just moved farther and farther away from God. Though we are not going to examine Cain and Abel, the flood, or the Tower of Babel in any detail, suffice it to say that each represents a qualitative step in the wrong direction.

So while God was hoping and waiting for mankind to reverse direction—or if not mankind, then at least a nation or two—His waiting seemed to be in vain.

Then, one day it happened. With the appearance of Abraham, hope for mankind had been rekindled. Abraham (as we have already seen on pages 16-20) was a person who was able to see through the veil cast by the myths and dogmas of his time, and make a clean break with the prevailing norms of consciousness. He was truly one of a kind. Abraham thought and lived differently from everyone else, and he was headed in the right direction.

The Mission: God and Abraham Strike a Deal

God wasn't about to let a golden opportunity slip through His fingers, and so He initiated a remarkable relationship with Abraham.

> *"And God said to Abraham; 'Lech Lecha, Go for yourself [not for Me] and leave your land, the community of your birth, your father's home and head for the land that I will show you. And I will transform you into a great nation and I will bless you, and make you well known and you will be a blessing. And those who bless you, I will bless; and those who curse you, I will curse—and blessing and goodness will come to all the families of the earth, through you."*

> Genesis 12:1-3

In Abraham, God saw the makings of mankind's way home. In Abraham, God saw a person who had the ability to raise a family that would grow into a nation capable of being a beacon for all the families and all the nations of the earth.

> *"And Abraham was ninety-nine years old when God appeared to him and said, 'I am the ultimate force in creation; walk before Me and represent Me with integrity. And I will set my Covenant between Me and between you and I will greatly increase you ... And I pledge My Covenant between Me and you and your offspring after you, throughout their generations—an eternal covenant—that I, God, will maintain a unique relationship with you and your descendants after you' ... And God said further to Abraham, 'and as for you, your obligation is to vigilantly preserve My Covenant, you as well as your descendants after you, forever.'"*
>
> Genesis 17:1-9

In this covenantal agreement between God and Abraham, we have the establishment of a two-way relationship—an indissoluble partnership—that on the one hand establishes Abraham's descendants as God's point men in the world, while also committing God to using the totality of His absolute power to aid and support them in that endeavor. And the whole purpose of this partnership was nothing less than to remedy all the damage left in Adam's wake, and to lead humanity to its ultimate purpose. Eventually, all the goodness, benefit, and blessing that God had intended for Adam and his descendants would at last find its way to humanity through Abraham and his descendants.

> *"This covenant imposed binding obligations on both parties involved. Abraham herein committed himself to becoming God's partner in both the repairing of creation and moving it to its final destiny."*
>
> Malbim, 19th century Biblical commentator

It was with this uniquely outstanding human being, Abraham, that God entered into a covenant, and it was with the sealing of this covenant that history would begin a wide turn in the right direction. Though this turn would prove to be so wide that at times history did little more than creep along, still, the momentum created by Abraham and affirmed by God was so powerful that there was no stopping its ultimate success.

Next Stop, Mount Sinai

The enlightenment achieved by Abraham and the profound relationship with God that this led to would become a guiding light for all humanity. Like a ship guided through the night's dense fog by the distant glow from a lighthouse, the people that would eventually be the heirs to God's Covenant with Abraham would serve as a guiding light through the frighteningly dark nights of human history.

From this point in the Torah, from the establishment of the covenant between God and Abraham, until the closing lines of God's book, the recording of early world history becomes very Judaeocentric.

Together, God and Abraham planted the seeds that would one day restore the beauty of a long-forgotten garden. But first, that plant had to take root and grow. And grow it did. Through the life of Abraham and his wife Sarah, continuing with their son Isaac and his wife Rebecca, and all the way through the lives of their great-grandchildren who settled—and were eventually enslaved—in Egypt, the seed of the Covenant grew until one day it struck roots so deep that nothing could ever dislodge it.

Let's Head for the Hills, Fellas

As you may recall from Sunday school—or from Steven Spielberg's *The Prince of Egypt*—after God flattened the Egyptians with ten plagues and then finished them off with that old splitting-of-the-Red-Sea trick, He headed straight for the hills—Mount Sinai, to be exact. And Abraham's descendants were right there with Him, every step of the way.

While the original covenant was binding on Abraham and his descendants, God wanted those descendants to use their own free will to confirm their commitment to it. So, in the absence of a venue as majestic as Versailles or as dignified as the east lawn of the White House, God settled on a small mountain in the Sinai desert. What was about to happen at Mount Sinai was the ratification of the Covenant with the nation that had grown out of the family of Abraham and Sarah.

Let's listen in on the proceedings of the ratification:

Guess Who *We're* Meeting with Tomorrow?

> *"In the third month after the exodus of the Jews from Egypt, on this day, they came to the wilderness of Sinai ... And Moses ascended to God and God called to him from the mountain and told him what to say to [Abraham's descendants] the house of Jacob and the children of Israel. 'You saw what I did to the Egyptians ... and now if you will listen carefully and preserve My Covenant, then, as a nation, you will have a unique relationship with Me ...'"*

So Moses relayed God's words to the nation and prepared them to meet their Maker—literally.

> *"And on the morning of the third day there was tremendous thunder and lightning and clouds on the mountain—and there was an extraordinarily powerful and prolonged shofar blast—and the entire nation freaked out* [not a literal translation] *... and the presence of God, transcendent and absolute, descended onto the mountain."*

So at Sinai, God laid out everything He had to say. What He was communicating was the fine print of the original deal with Abraham, the spiritual details of the unique, mission-centered relationship known as the Covenant. Then, when He finished His communication, God instructed Moses to write everything down and present it to the nation for their signature.

> *"And Moses transcribed all the words of God. Then, in the morning, Moses got up and built a ratification altar at the foot of the mountain and twelve pillars representing each of the twelve tribes. He then sent the first-born of every family to present an offering on the altar. Finally, Moses took the book of the Covenant and read it to the nation, and they responded in unison— 'Whatever God says, we will do—and afterwards we'll try to understand as best we can.' At that point, Moses took a bit of blood from the altar and sprinkled it on the nation, and he said, 'This is the blood of the Covenant that God has sealed with you regarding all of these words.'"*

"And Afterwards We'll Try to Understand"

When the nation said, *"Whatever God says, we will do—and afterwards we'll try to understand,"* they not only signaled their readiness to willingly sign on to the Covenant, they simultaneously turned the clock of history back to the good old days in the garden. Where Adam had once thought that he could outsmart God, the nation charged with undoing all of the damage caused by Adam, now declared that it wouldn't make that same mistake. Whatever God said, this nation would do, and only afterwards would they try to make sense of God's communication. But in the end they all recognized that whether or not they understood, the path to the deepest possible attachment to God lay in the privilege of being His emissary and carrying out His wishes within creation.

The rest, as they say, is history.

> *"The history of Judaism and of the Jews is a long and complicated story, full of blood and tears. With all that, the Jews are still, essentially, the same stubborn, dedicated people, now, and forever maybe, affirming the same three things. First, they are a people of the law as given in the holy books of Moses. Second, they are the*

chosen people of God, having an eternal covenant with Him. Third, they are a witness that God is and will be forevermore."

Charles Van Doren, associate director of the Institute for Philosophical Research, *A History of Knowledge*[27]

So Who is Debbie?

Debbie is you and I—the descendants of Abraham and Sarah, the descendants of the nation that encountered God at Sinai, and the ones upon whom God Himself is counting on to finish cleaning up Adam's mess and finally reveal the beauty of His garden.

God after

Death

5

We All Live, We All Die, We All ...

If you are reading these words, then you are alive. Similarly, if you are reading these words, then you will also die. Don't get me wrong, I hope this inevitability is a long way down the road—for all of us—but the truth of the matter is, that while they say that death and taxes are two things no one can escape, they're wrong. People can and do escape paying taxes; it's death that's the really tough one.

King Sarnac the Gentle

There was a man who lived about 4,300 years ago in Mesopotamia by the name of Ubar the Great. Unlike Alexander the Great, who would not appear on the stage of history for another two millennia, Ubar the Great earned his epitaph because he was considered to be the kindest man the world had ever known. Legend had it that whenever people smiled in the world, there flashed in their minds the image of Ubar. Very few specifics are known of this man's life, though it seems he had a mentor. In one of the fragments of stories that remains about Ubar the Great, he himself makes passing mention of someone named Sarnac. For years, most scholars thought that the name Sarnac meant "vision of beauty and goodness" and that Sarnac was an actual person who had in some way inspired Ubar the Great to live life the way he did. Recent findings have led many scholars to the conclusion that the correct meaning of the word Sarnac is "king of beauty and goodness" and that in fact he may have been the head of a tribe or even a lost pre-Mesopotamian civilization that valued goodness as the ultimate beauty and highest of human pursuits.

What an enchanting notion. Perhaps there was a time in our murky past when there arose a civilization that honored above all others the good, kind and gentle person and not the warrior, conqueror and slayer of men who has been so universally esteemed throughout the ages. And what a pity. What a tragic pity that Sarnac, his civilization, and all the wonderfully beautiful people who populated that place have been forever forgotten. At best, they are a speculative footnote to history; though, in fact, they are gone. Their ideas and teachings are gone, their culture is gone, and so too their deeds—their countless edifices to virtue and goodness—all of these have been swept away by the merciless winds of time that have made faceless dust of them and who knows how much more of our past.

We Are All the Dust of the Future

Now here's a happy thought for you: we all live, we all die, and eventually we are *all* reduced to faceless dust. Sooner or later, who we were, how we lived, and what we accomplished will be simply and totally forgotten. Eventually nothing whatsoever will remain of us. Not even the whisper of a faint memory.

Let's imagine for a moment that the answer to the question of what happens after you die is nothing, absolutely nothing. You rot, decay, turn into a worm's lunch and that's it; you're gone forever. If this were the case with death, what implications would this have for life?

Let's think about this in the context of the creation of a great work of art and its creator. For example, let's think about what is arguably the most famous painting in the world, the Mona Lisa, and its creator, Leonardo da Vinci. Let's try and put ourselves in Leonardo's shoes and see how we would respond if confronted with the hypothetical situation as follows:

Scenario # 1.

You are putting the final touches on the smile of the Mona Lisa. Throughout the time spent on this painting, you have employed musicians and entertainers to keep your model amused so that she would always maintain that special smile. Then, one night, you have a dream. In your dream, an angel appears to you and tells you that this painting will be studied and admired by millions of people for hundreds of years to come. Unfortunately, the angel also tells you that after six hundred years a terrible fire will break out in the Louvre (the angel gave you a tour of the Louvre in a different dream) that will reduce your masterpiece to ashes.

The question is this: Does your knowledge that your work will only last for five or six hundred years diminish your commitment to the project? Do you find yourself less enthusiastic about its completion or its quality, because it is doomed to the dust bin of history? Or are you inspired to persevere knowing that your work will not only endure for centuries but that it will make an impression on millions of people from around the world?

Scenario # 2.

You are about halfway through the four or five years that it will take you to complete this painting. You have poured your heart and soul, along with all the talent and creativity you can muster, into this effort. Then, one day, your wealthy patron walks in and tells you that he plans to destroy the painting the moment you announce its completion. "Work on, my dear Leonardo," he says, "but know that the moment you complete this work, I will have it tossed into a fire where both you and I and the woman who has sat for so long will watch it go up in flames. Why, you ask? Because that is my wish, as well as the price for my continued support of your efforts. Now go ahead and paint on, my dear friend."

The question is this: Does your patron's announcement of his intentions to destroy your painting in any way affect your relationship to this creative effort? Are you less motivated than before? Are you less able to summon the same inner resources that have driven your effort until now? Do you perhaps feel like just rushing through the rest of the painting in order to get the job over with as quickly as possible? Or, perhaps, the completed painting itself is enough to justify your investment of years of creative toil whether or not it will endure for more than a day and whether or not it will ever be seen by anyone other than yourself, your patron, and Mrs. Lisa herself.

Though I can't speak for Mr. da Vinci, I suspect that most people would be far more motivated and capable of completing the Mona Lisa to the best of their ability if they knew it would have an enduring impact rather than if it would be lost to oblivion as soon as it was completed. And while it's true that the artist can never be stripped of the knowledge and satisfaction of having invested the absolute best of himself in a creative effort, would not the prospect of the immediate destruction of the fruits of that effort be the greatest challenge one could possibly face on the road to completion?

If the answer to the question "What happens after you die?" is 'Nothing,' then isn't life, at best, scenario number one, and in most instances, much closer to something like scenario number two? Think about it. If what's left of us after death is nothingness—no existence, awareness, consciousness, or memories—not even the memories that others have of us, then what does this tell us about our life's accomplishments? Even if we are the creators of a Mona Lisa, a masterpiece, and even if this masterpiece is in the form of a beautiful family, a classic film, or the founding of a soup kitchen that feeds thousands of hungry people, in the end are we not all Sarnac? In a thousand years, two hundred years, or perhaps in just a matter of weeks after our deaths, won't all of our accomplishments be reduced to nothing but faceless dust? And if it's true that our planet has many hundreds of millions of years to go until the big bang ends in a big crunch, and if it's also true that the planet we inhabit is less in proportion to the universe than a grain of sand is to all the beaches on earth, then doesn't this reduce all of us—our births and deaths, our lives, efforts, accomplishments, and legacies—to being no more than a bit of dust that was born, lived, died, and forgotten in the blink of an eye? Does anything in life really matter—how much meaning can there be to anything in life—if all we are is faceless bits of dust whose meanderings will quickly and inevitably be lost and forgotten for all eternity?

Rosh Hashanah

Rosh Hashanah, the holiday that marks the Jewish New Year, is known as the Day of Judgment. This is the day when God's court is in session, so to speak, and He judges the deeds and lives of all people.

Tell me, do you not detest being in the presence of a judgmental person? Is there nothing more unsettling than knowing that your actions are being scrutinized by others? Isn't being subjected to a process of review, evaluation, and judgment absolutely the pits?

When it comes to God, just the opposite is true. That God judges us is the surest sign that there exists a meaningful relationship between the Designer and Creator of the universe and His creations—each and every one of us.

Everyone knows that life is either meaningless, that our existence amounts to nothing more than a sandcastle waiting to be washed away, or that life is meaningful. The judgment of Rosh Hashanah says emphatically that life is meaningful. Who we are, what we do and achieve, the efforts that we make—all of this—matters to God Himself. While Jews have always approached Rosh Hashanah with the utmost seriousness, it is also a festival, a day for celebrating our relationship with God in light of the awareness that He cares deeply about how things are going.

If you want to destroy a child, don't beat her, ignore her. To a child, the most devastating response to how she acts is no response at all. A parent who doesn't react to a report card, to behavior, or to the choice of friends or rented videos is a parent who is sending a clear message. And that most destructive of all messages is this: I'm not interested. I really couldn't care one way or the other about you—about who you are, how you live, or what you do or don't do with your life. Disinterest is the opposite of relationship.

The message that Rosh Hashanah sends, and the message that we celebrate, is this: the relationship is real, my choices and their consequences are of paramount importance, and God cares because I matter.

More to Life Than Heaven and Hell

Remember, creation is for us, and the deepest meaning of this is that we were created with the potential for a relationship with our Creator. Jewish tradition and teaching has always maintained that this relationship outlives the life of the body. So does this mean that Judaism believes in heaven and hell, in eternal reward, or the flames of eternal damnation? Not exactly. What Judaism believes in is a relationship. In the Jewish way of thinking all reward and punishment is in terms of depth versus superficiality in our relationship with God. It's either a close relationship, or it isn't.

So you mean heaven is a really great relationship and hell is a lousy, dysfunctional one? Sort of, but it's a bit more involved than that.

The relationship that is inherent in the act of Creation is a relationship that is as enduring as the Creator Himself; yet, like a marriage, it doesn't happen overnight. It takes time to develop and deepen the relationship. There is a process involved, a journey—from getting to know one another, to engagement, to the marriage itself, and beyond. To all the depth and closeness that can only come with time, effort, commitment, and a shared life. The relationship between a human being and the Creator also takes time and effort. This, as you will recall, is because if we achieve it as a result of no choice or effort of our own, if it's just handed to us, then how real, deep, and pleasurable can it actually be? The road to achieving actual being through a relationship with God is a process that begins with life and continues along a continuum that looks like this—

Life

The essence of human existence, of life, lies in our free will—in our being created "in the image of God." As God is independent and creative, so we have the potential to live freely, to make our own choices, and ultimately to create our own lives. The world and every individual within it is a masterpiece in waiting. It is the great challenge and opportunity inherent in free will that separates us from a rhinoceros or an apple tree. The rhinoceros doesn't *choose* to charge when threatened. It just does so because that's the way it was programmed. So too the apple tree; all it can ever do is what it was programmed to do—give apples. But people are different. We make choices—to dominate or to comfort, to share or to withhold, to be kind or cruel, destructive or life giving. Ultimately, we choose to face reality or to hide from it, to respond and relate to God, or to ignore Him.

But there is a problem: life is difficult.

Life is difficult and uncomfortable and painful and frustrating and unsettling and full of disappointment and suffering. So often all that we are reaching for in life seems to be dangling just beyond our reach. So we have a sense, there must be more, life must be part of a continuum. The life that we experience in this physical existence is one that is custom designed and perfectly balanced for the operation of our free will. From the time we are born until our last day on earth, we live in a dimension that allows us to achieve the greatest possible connection to God through sheer will, effort, earning, and having as little as possible given to us for nothing. It is the inescapable need for us to freely choose and earn that closeness with God that necessitates an environment that is both supportive and fiercely oppositional.

Life as we are aware of it in the physical world is the beginning of the process of relationship. However, it is more than just one of many steps in the process; it is the most pivotal aspect of the entire process. It is only while we are alive in the blended form of physical and spiritual, in a world that is simultaneously supportive and oppositional, that we can make real choices that have actual consequences. And it is these choices that set the stage for the future of the relationship. Once we are divested of our free will, once our being is no longer conflicted and our environment no longer a source of dissonance, then all we can do is live with the consequences of our choices, because choice itself will no longer exist.

Death of the Body

So death, or more precisely the death of the body, is the termination of free will. As such, death is far more than the cessation of vital physical and chemical functions. Death is the separation of the body from the soul and the conclusion of our existence as free-willed beings. It is a point along the continuum of existence.

Gone with the Wind, the 1960 World Series, and Other Great Endings

To fully appreciate the Jewish understanding of what comes after death, it will be helpful to consider the following dialogue recorded in the Talmud:

"The Roman emperor Marcus Aurelius once asked Rabbi Judah the Prince [the pre-eminent scholar of his day], 'Is it not true that the body and the soul can conspire to exempt one another from any type of heavenly judgment? It would work like this: The body [when it is called in for judgment] will say, "Just look at me. Ever since death I have just been lying there like a helpless stone. Clearly, the only reason I was ever involved in any wrongdoing was because the soul gave me the ability to act as I did; so if anyone should be held accountable, it's the soul." However, the soul will then reply, "Look at me. Ever since I have been separated from the body I have been flying like a bird above the surface of the world—I never really had any interest in the physical world. It was the body that led me to do the things I did."'

"Rabbi Judah's reply was in the form of a parable. 'Marcus my friend, consider the following analogy:

'Once there was a king who had a magnificent orchard full of the most delectable and valuable figs. To protect his orchard, the king hired two guards, one who was blind and another who was a cripple. One day, the cripple said to the blind man, "These are truly beautiful figs, why don't you put me on your shoulders and I will direct you so that we can pick and enjoy some figs." And that is just what they did. Later, when the king returned and saw what had happened, he demanded to know where his figs had gone. At that point the cripple said, "I couldn't have taken them, I can't even walk!" And the blind man said, "I can't see! How could I have possibly taken the figs?"

'So what was the king's response? He took the cripple, sat him on the shoulders of the blind man and proclaimed— "Now what do you have to say for yourselves?"'"

This is a story about the granddaddy of all Rosh Hashanahs. It's about final judgment and ultimate responsibility for one's actions.

While a post-death day of reckoning may conjure up hair-raising visions worthy of Dante himself, Jews have always understood this parable to be saying something fundamental about the actualization of the relationship between people and God. It says that God doesn't forget about us after we die; it says that God continues to care about us after we die, and most importantly, it says that God continues to relate to us after we die. In other words, just as the judgment of Rosh Hashanah implies concern and caring (a relationship) so too God's future day of judgment, His reaction to the totality of our lives, implies an intimate relationship that transcends death.

So does this mean that Judaism actually believes in some kind of life after death? That in some way the soul and the body have continued existence and awareness even after they have been separated by death?

That's right, and if you think about it, the reality couldn't be different.

Resurrection of the Dead

The free-willed being who lives, and breathes, and confronts all the challenges of forging a relationship with the Creator is a unique being comprised of body and soul. That's what we human beings are. As such, who is it that is struggling, and choosing and trying to create a relationship with the Creator? Is it the body? The soul? Neither, or both? The Jewish understanding is that it is both. It is the totality of the human being, which is body and soul together. Thus, the achievement of the ultimate closeness to God can only be in terms of the complete human being—body and soul together.

It is for this reason that Judaism sees the ultimate reunification of the body and the soul as the only way that the purpose of existence can be fulfilled. *We* are the ones whom God created with the potential to have the supreme pleasure of a relationship with Him, and we are a soul *and* a body.

The relationship continuum that begins with birth and then travels through life and death culminates in the future state of existence known as resurrection. This is a state of being that is unlike anything we can possibly imagine. We live in a world of striving and becoming. That future world is one of ultimate achievement and actualization. While in some way these two worldly places have something in common, in essence they are utterly different. Our sages call this future state of being *olam haba*, "the world to come," and they compare it to the Sabbath, the day of rest.

> *"One who makes the effort to prepare for the Sabbath will have something to eat on the Sabbath."*
>
> Talmud

> *"The Sabbath is a slight approximation of* olam haba, *the world to come."*
>
> Talmud

In these statements, the sages are telling us that there is a dimension to the Sabbath that goes far beyond its being a day of rest or even a day for spiritual renewal. It's a taste, a whiff of the ultimate. According to Jewish law, one must refrain from all forms of creative labor on the Sabbath. Additionally, on the Sabbath there is an incredible obligation to "view all of one's unfinished projects as if they had already been completed." So what the weekly experience of the Sabbath creates (among other things) is an encounter with the ultimate state of being—when the relationship is no longer being formed and nurtured but has finally reached its fullest fruition.

So after Death We Just Hang Around Waiting for Resurrection?

Not exactly.

While Jewish tradition does discuss what takes place after death and prior to the resurrection, the truth is, since it is a state of existence unlike any we can relate to and since no one has come back with a definitive report about what transpires, we can only speak about it in general and somewhat vague terms.

In general, our tradition has it that what takes place after death is some sort of a purification process that readies the body and the soul for their eventual reunification. The goal of this process is to enable them, together, to partake of the relationship they created in the world prior to death (known as *olam hazeh*, "this world").

This purification process works roughly, very roughly, like this:

Imagine a fictitious fellow named Al Mercer who was successful in business and who, in 1967 at the age of thirty-eight, put together a group of investors to purchase the New York Yankees. Then, for the rest of his life he did nothing other than manage his investment. He was either with the team or involved in team business every day. He was at spring training and at meetings about trades and salaries and free agents. He was there when the manager was deciding who to keep on the roster and who to cut, and in all of these matters, he was more than just there—he was totally involved. In fact, he always had the last say. From who would manage to who would pitch in the first game of a World Series, he always reserved the right to make the call. In short, everyone knew what the newspapers proclaimed, "Al Mercer *is* the New York Yankees."

Then, one day, Mr. Mercer's soul slipped out of his body and Yankee fans across the country were deeply saddened.

Now let's think about this particular body and soul. While they were partnered together in the form of Al Mercer, they were constantly at odds with one another. Al's soul felt that it had the potential to build something great, something that could touch the lives of millions of people. And Al was a man of vision and drive and talent. He really could have made a difference in this world. But then there was Al's body. It wasn't quite as ambitious as Al's soul. It had other interests and other goals. It wanted Al to pursue achievements that weren't quite as difficult as his soul had in mind. And while Al certainly did do a number of wonderful things in his lifetime, in the overall scheme of things, it was his body that called the most important shots. In the end, when the world asked, "Who was Al Mercer?" the answer was "Al Mercer *was* the New York Yankees."

So after the funeral, after all the tributes had been fondly spoken, and after Al had been inducted into the Hall of Fame, what was left of him? Well, what was left was his body and soul, and both of them were in for a rude awakening. When reflecting back on their pre-death existence, what Al's body and soul realized was that what Al had become in life was a baseball team, which isn't the worst thing in the world, but it also wasn't anywhere near what Al could have become.

And that's the purification process that takes place after death. After death, the unencumbered soul clearly saw the potential that it knew Al possessed all along. It saw the true greatness that was within its reach, if only Al hadn't given in to his body's agenda. At this point, the soul was in a state of anguish at having missed an irretrievable opportunity—truly the opportunity of a lifetime.

In some way, the fact that the soul's agenda took a back seat to the body's did damage to the soul. It is the undeniable recognition of all that wasted potential that repairs the damage. At the same time, the body too has its own moment of truth. When separated from the soul, the body realizes the shallow and fleeting nature of everything it fought so hard for in life. Everything that it had relentlessly pushed for was now gone. It could never be touched, never be sensed, nor experienced again. As the body experiences an awareness of its own decay, it simultaneously realizes that everything it had ever pursued was also doomed to decay. And that's painful. And that painful awareness is the body's own purification process.

According to Jewish tradition, this purification process lasts for, at most, twelve months. After that, the soul resides in some sort of a spiritual retreat center where it internalizes its realization and waits for the day when it will be reunited with its old buddy and finally be able to have what it had been longing for all along. Unfortunately, however, its ultimate potential, the depth of closeness to the Creator that it will later experience, will ultimately be defined by the way it had originally lived. In the end, the new and improved Al Mercer will experience a degree of pleasure, connection and closeness to God that is beyond anything we can imagine. It will be a spiritual existence unlike anything we know of. But it won't be quite what it could have been.

can God give Himself a cold so bad, even He

Can't cure it?

6

The Passover Principle: Go Ahead, Ask!

"*Mah nishtana*—Why is this night different from all other nights ..."

It is difficult to think of a more universally recognized Jewish phrase than the *mah nishtana*, the four questions asked by children at the Passover Seder. It is quite telling that the context for these famous four questions, the Passover seder, is considered to be the primary vehicle for transmitting Judaism from one generation to the next. It is testimony to the fact that Judaism encourages questioning and sees the nurturing of a thoughtful mind as a key to its continuity and vitality. So let's look at four questions of our own, and, rest assured, God won't mind.

I. Can God Give Himself a Cold That Even He Can't Cure?

This question is directed at the idea that God has no limitations and is therefore all-powerful. The question is this: If God can, in fact, give Himself an incurable cold, then obviously He is not all-powerful, because He can't even take care of His own sniffles. On the other hand, if God can't give Himself *that* bad of a cold, then His power is again limited by the fact that He can't give Himself anything worse than the common curable cold.

Don't Trip over God's Ankle

This question exists because someone forgot to read the warning label on page 12. An almost inevitable pitfall of talking about God is that we can't help but speak—and therefore think and conceive—of God in human terms. Remember, whenever we apply terms like "speaking" or "thinking" to God, we are speaking metaphorically. In truth, God never "spoke" a word in His life, and for that matter, He doesn't even have a life. You see, when we say the word "speak," our minds automatically conjure up an image that includes lips, vocal cords, and sound. But God has no lips and no vocal cords with which to make any sounds. Not only that, He *can't* have lips, because if God had lips He would then be physical in nature, and like all things physical, He would be subject to the limitations of physical matter and space. In short, He wouldn't be God anymore.

So, is there anything God can't do? Yes, He can't not be God. He can't be a crocodile, a centipede, or even a man. Remember, God's existence is absolutely independent of all He created. Any existence that has anything to do with time, space, or matter, by definition, has nothing to do with God. The moment we speak in terms of an existence that is within the bounds of time and space, we know for sure that we can't be speaking about God.

So, can God give Himself a cold so severe even He can't cure it? No. Because colds belong to the world of the physical and God doesn't.

II. Isn't God Too Busy to Care about a Little Guy Like Me?

The problem here is that we are caught up in trying to look at the world through God's eyes, while unavoidably using our own perceptions. This means that for us, who are finite and limited, it's impossible to relate to every facet of life with the same weight of importance. We have to prioritize. However, to God, everything that exists does so only because God wants it to exist as a part of the entirety of creation. To God, it's all meaningful and important or He wouldn't bring it into existence in the first place. And He has the ability to be intimately concerned about and involved with everything He creates because—well—because He's God.

It's important to mention an additional idea here.

It's true that to God everything that exists is of inestimable value. At the same time there are matters of greater and lesser value. The Jewish understanding of creation is that it has a purpose and that, within creation, certain elements are the purpose of creation and others are facilitators of that purpose. Human beings and their free-willed ability to be connected to God are the purpose of creation. Oak trees, on the other hand, while they are not the purpose of creation, do, inasmuch as they provide shade, beauty, and lumber for people, make a meaningful contribution to the purpose of creation. So, while God can and does "care" about everything in creation more than we can ever imagine, He cares about each and every one of us even more than that. And this is why, no matter how busy we may imagine Him to be, He's never too busy for any of us.

III. If God Already Knows the Outcome of an Election, Did the Winning Candidate Really Have a Choice Whether or Not to Run?

Human beings have free will—not!

Earlier, when we discussed the issues of body and soul, free will and "the image of God," we wrote, *When it comes to the tension between the disparate elements of our being, we are free to choose as we like. We may choose to do what we want to do or we may choose to do what we feel like doing, but in either case, the choice is ours.*

The problem, however, is that God knows what we are going to choose even before we choose it; He knows what we are going to do before we do it and He knows everything that is going to ever happen before it actually happens. So if God already knows what I am going to choose, doesn't this foreknowledge mean, in essence, that all my choices have already been made?

Human beings do *not* have free will—not!

In the words of Maimonides, the answer to this question is "broader than the earth is broad and deeper than the sea is deep." I take this to mean that even if I owned a thousand pens (or at least six laser printer cartridges), I could never do justice to addressing this question. So I won't even try. What I will do, however, is point out that, once again, we have tripped over that bothersome anthropomorphic warning label. You see, the question itself is actually flawed.

If you think about this question, and at the same time keep in mind God's nonrelationship to time, you will begin to see the flaw in the question. The most straightforward way to put the question is this: If God knows today what I will choose to do tomorrow, then when tomorrow arrives, will I really have a choice?

The problem is God *doesn't* know today what you are going to do tomorrow because for God there is no today and tomorrow (or yesterday for that matter). Since God's existence is independent of time, His "knowledge" is also independent of time. You see, when we reflect on the nature of our own knowledge, we find that it is linked up with time. If you learn something new today, if in any way you acquire a new bit of knowledge or understanding, then you can say that you know more today than you knew yesterday. In conceiving of one's knowledge, one always simultaneously thinks in terms of now or before or later, and all of these are aspects of time.

God, however, is different. And that's the whole point. Just as He is different from us, so is His knowledge different from ours. We naturally assume that if knowledge exists today about what will happen tomorrow then there is a connection between today's knowledge and tomorrow's events. This might be so of human knowledge, but not of God's knowledge. God's knowledge isn't related to time, isn't affected by time, and has no causal impact on time. Therefore, human beings have free will.

For more on this issue I suggest taking up a study of Maimonides, but make sure to bring along a bathing suit, because it's an issue that is "deeper than the sea."

epilogue: follow the "light"
a kabbalistic
Retrospective

7

Kabbalah is the deepest dimension of the Torah. It's where the finest subtleties of God's wisdom are to be found, and it's easily misunderstood. Like the world of quantum mechanics, the realm of *kabbalah* deals with a concealed dimension of reality and often employs words and concepts that have meanings radically different from those we are used to in everyday life.

The following essay is only the slightest glimpse of an aspect of the Torah as it emerges in the kabbalistic tradition. The topic of this essay is light, but it's not the kind of light we're accustomed to. It's an altogether different sort of light, a spiritual "light" that has the quality of illumination, but not in the physical sense. This isn't a light that brightens a dark room; rather, this is a light that is present within the hidden essence of all existence, life, and history.

This essay follows the general outline of the book you have just read while looking at the flow of ideas and events from a different perspective—the perspective of "light." As you read, you will notice bold text. These are quotes from the body of this book and are there to provide a sense of balance and continuity.

Follow the "Light"

God, "Light," and Relationship

> That creation is for us means that we have the potential to be intimately connected to our Creator—to God—through a relationship.

When God created, He did far more than just bring endless stuff into existence. The essence of creation is the creation of the possibility for something other than God to experience God. Creation is what makes relationship possible.

The possibility of relationship means that there must exist two parties to the relationship. As they say, "It takes two to tango."

The relationship that lies at the core of creation, the relationship of the human being to God, begins with the creation of "light." This term, "light," is not to be confused with the kind of light that comes from flashlights, stars, and photons ... it's not the kind of light that dispels darkness, rather, the original "light" of creation is a reference to God being manifest in creation in a way that He can be related to.

Consider the following accounts of the creation of "light" and light.

Creation: Day one

> *"In the beginning God created the heaven and the earth. The earth was unformed and void, and darkness was upon the surface of the depths; the Presence of God hovered above the surface of the water. God said, 'Let there be light' and there was light."*

Genesis 1:1-3

Creation: Day four

> *"God said, 'Let there be lights in the expanse of heaven to separate between the day and the night.' And God made two great lights, the greater light for dominion in the day, and the lesser light for dominion at night, as well as the stars."*

Genesis 1:14-16

Clearly, there was a creation of some kind of light on the first day of creation that was altogether different from the light of the sun and the moon that was created on the fourth day. The question is just exactly what was this "light" before light?

In kabbalah, the epiphany of creation is termed *ohr aiyn sof*, which means "the appearance of God's light." The instant of creation is the birth of relationship, and this birth is expressed by the word "light." The expression and manifestation of God in creation is called "light."

Without light, life is not possible. The same is true of "light." Without it, there is no possibility of life. The "light" of God is what makes existence not only possible, but meaningful. More than just what sustains life, God's "light" is what elevates life. It's what creates the possibility for spirituality, and it's what places a relationship with God within the reach of every human being.

God Is One, And So Is "Light"

In seeking God, we seek what is known in Hebrew as *echad*, the oneness and unity of actual, absolute being.

The *Shema*—"*Listen O' Israel, God our Lord, God is One*"—is the ultimate Jewish statement of what life is all about. Life is about the potential relationship with *echad*, with God. It has been observed that the *Shema* contains twenty-five letters, and it just happens that the word "light" is the twenty-fifth word in the Torah. (By the way, "light" was also created on the twenty-fifth day of the month of *Elul*, and the holiday of Chanukah—the festival of lights—begins on the twenty-fifth day of the month of *Kislev*.)

The number twenty-five, it turns out, is a very significant number. As a rule, where you find allusions to twenty-five in the Torah, you also find God, and "light."

Keep this significance of twenty-five in mind as you read further.

Adam and the Hidden "Light"

> Adam possessed an intense awareness of God ... Adam knew
> that he had almost limitless potential ... Adam didn't
> realize how much distance would actually be created by a
> seemingly small departure from God's wishes. In fact,
> the distance that Adam created was disastrous,
> not only for himself but for the entire world.

The Talmudic tradition regarding the original "light" is that its presence in the world was short-lived. In fact, the Talmud tells us that the "light" was apparent within creation for just thirty-six hours, and then it was hidden. The question, of course, is why was the "light" hidden? And the answer is that in hiding the "light," God was creating a cosmic framework for the fundamental dynamic of man's existence; it's called hide-and-seek.

God's "light" was hidden just enough to make it not overwhelmingly apparent. As a result, man would not be irresistibly drawn to the "light." It was this hiding of the "light," therefore, that set the stage for Adam, the first human being.

As we have already seen, Adam didn't fare so well.

Now, let's look at God's response to Adam's failure:

> *"And they [Adam and Eve] heard the voice of God
> manifesting itself throughout the garden, at the approach
> of evening, and the man and his wife hid from God,
> amongst the trees of the garden. And God called out to
> the man, and said to him, 'Where are you?'"*

Genesis 3:8-9

Is it possible that God didn't know where Adam was? Clearly not. Rather, within these words lies a veiled message. According to the sages, the Hebrew word used to express "where are you?"—*ayekah*—is a highly unusual word, so unusual in fact that it is actually an allusion to the hidden "light."

Consider the following and remember, the original "light" was manifest for just thirty-six hours before being hidden.

"Rabbi Shimon the son of Pazi said, 'The numerical value of ayekah *["where are you"] is thirty-six.'"*

Midrash Zuta, Eichah 1:1

And further:

"The word light appears thirty-six times in the Torah."

Rokeach

When God called out to Adam and said, *"ayekoh*, where are you?" what He was actually doing was pointing out to Adam the consequences of his action. The deeper meaning of *ayekoh* is, "Where is the light?"* God was telling Adam that he had allowed an enormous opportunity to slip through his fingers.

"Adam," God was saying, "you had a chance, by virtue of your free will, to reveal the hidden 'light,' and you missed your chance. Adam, when I hid the 'light,' I was creating the potential for a fully genuine relationship—a relationship that wouldn't be imposed but would be freely embraced. In hiding the 'light,' I actually gave you the possibility for closeness, and instead, you created distance. You could have revealed the 'light,' but now, Adam—*ayekoh*! Where is the 'light?'"

And so the "light" remained hidden—hidden, but not extinguished.

Abraham Is Light

With the appearance of Abraham, hope for mankind had been rekindled. Abraham was able to see through the veil...

As a result of Adam's failure, the "light" remained hidden, and it would take another two millennia before someone would arise with the potential to reveal it. That person was Abraham, and Abraham was a man who was more than enlightened—he was light itself.

---

*The word *ayekoh* can be split into two words. *Aye*, which means "where" and *koh*, which is a difficult word to translate and seems to have different meanings in different contexts. However, the numerical value of the word *koh* is twenty-five, the number that represents "light." When looked at this way, the word *ayekoh* literally means, "where is the light?"

"The earth was unformed and void, and darkness was upon the surface of the depths... and God said, 'Let there be light.'"

Genesis 1:2-3

"Abraham is the light. The generations preceding Abraham were unformed and darkness, and Abraham was the light of existence."

Maharal, Gevuros 5:34

And of course, Abraham had an encounter with twenty-five—with the hidden "light."

To grow to the point where he would be able to utilize all of his abilities, Abraham had to face ten tests. With each successive test, Abraham came a step closer to actualizing his potential for bringing "light" into the world.

By the end, as Abraham and his son Isaac were approaching the place of his final test, the Torah says—*"And Abraham said to the young men accompanying him, 'Stay here with the donkey while the lad [Isaac] and I go there.'"* What's interesting is that the Hebrew word used here for "there," *koh*, is an unusual word. But the use of this strange word is no mistake. In fact, it's an allusion to something else—the "light." You see, this is the same word, with the same numerical value of twenty-five, that appeared in the story of Adam. So when Abraham said that he and Isaac would go *koh*, "there," what he was actually saying was that he and Isaac would go *koh*, "to the light."

God now had an answer to His question. God said to Adam, *ayeh-koh*, "Where is the light?" Two thousand years later the answer came back: the "light" is with Abraham.

Moses, Torah, and the Hidden "Light"

Eventually, the goodness and blessing that God had intended for Adam and his descendants would at last find its way to humanity through Abraham and his descendants.

From the seed of Abraham grew the family and then the people of Israel. This people soon found itself enslaved in a very, very dark place—a place called Egypt.

In Hebrew, the word for Egypt, *Mitzrayim*, means "tight, restricted, and closed in."

On the one hand, this restrictive aspect of Egypt refers to the fact that it was impossible for prisoners and slaves to escape its borders. On a deeper level, however, Egypt was a spiritual black hole, a place from which nothing could escape, not even light itself.

Abraham had bequeathed the potential for "light" to his descendants, but now Egypt was threatening to smother it. Only with the appearance of Moses, and then the giving of the Torah, would the potential revelation of the "light" be assured.

The transformation of Moses from a prince in the house of Pharoah to the savior of the Jewish people is captured by two verses in the Torah.

> *"And Moses grew up and went out to his brothers and saw their burdens, and he saw an Egyptian beating one of his Jewish brothers. And he turned here and there (koh v'koh) and he saw that there was no man, so he struck the Egyptian and hid him in the sand."*

> Exodus 2:11-12

There it is again. That same strange word, *koh*, and that same number, twenty-five. Moses is to be the one who will lead the Jewish people out of the place of restricted light, and how does his career begin? With a turn to *koh*, a turn toward the "light."

> *"When Moses was born, the entire house became filled with light."*

> Rashi

Moses, like Abraham, was a man of "light," and eventually he would lead the Jewish people to a "light" of their own.

> *"With the hidden light, God nourishes the world."*

> Zohar

"For the commandment is a candle, and the Torah is light."

Proverbs 6:23

"The light created on the first day was hidden in the Torah itself."

Baal Shem Tov, founder of Chassidism

Could it be that the Torah itself is the repository for the original hidden "light" of creation? Could it be that the "light" hidden by God, the "light" that Adam failed to reveal—the "light" of connection between God and man—is now hidden in the Torah? Consider what happened to Moses after his encounter on Mount Sinai.

"When Moses descended from Mount Sinai—and in the hand of Moses were the two tablets of testimony when he descended from the mountain—Moses did not realize that the skin of his face had become radiant from speaking to Him."

Exodus 34:29

With the experience of receiving the Torah from God Himself, Moses became, quite literally, a radiant light.

It seems that while the "light" may be hidden, it is far from lost. In fact, the same vessel that contains the hidden "light" is the vehicle for its revelation.

Operation "Light" Up the World

The covenant between God and the Jewish people that was sealed at Mount Sinai is embodied in the Torah and so is the "light."

"The hidden light from the first day of creation was restored and revealed through the first set of tablets."

Rabbi Isaac Luria, 16th century mystic

Adam was unable to reveal God's "light" in the world. As a result, the entire purpose of creation was left hanging in abeyance. From the time of Adam onwards, it was as if all of creation were holding its breath waiting for another path to open up and finally reveal the "light." What creation was waiting for was Sinai.

> *"And it was evening, and it was morning, a second day... and it was evening, and it was morning, a third day ... and it was evening, and it was morning, a fourth day ... and it was evening, and it was morning, the sixth day."*
>
> Genesis

> *"The sixth day is an allusion to the sixth day of the month of Sivan, the day of the giving of the Torah. For, from the time of the sixth day of creation, all of creation knew that its fate was dependent on what would happen on a future sixth day, the sixth of Sivan."*
>
> Rashi, Genesis 1:31

The sixth day of creation was both the day on which the first human beings were created and the day on which they failed to reveal the "light." The sixth day of Sivan was both the day on which the Jewish people accepted the Torah and the day which would provide a way for the "light" to shine.

After Sinai, the challenge that was Adam's fell on the shoulders of the Jewish people.

> *"I am God; I called you for the purpose of righteousness... and I made you a Covenant people, to be a light to the nations."*
>
> Isaiah 42:6

> *"The purpose of creation could not be fulfilled until the Jewish nation left Egypt and received the Torah at Sinai. It was then that they would achieve the potential for being a 'light to the nations' and bring an awareness of God to the entire world."*
>
> Netziv, Introduction to Exodus

In the End—"Light"

After eating from the tree of the knowledge of good and evil, God came down pretty hard on Adam and Eve. In addition to telling them that they would now have to die and be buried in the ground, God also told them that they would have to toil like never before just to eke out a living and that from that point forth childbearing would be a difficult and painful experience. When God finished telling them all about the terrible consequences of their actions, the following happened—

> "And God made for Adam and his wife garments of skin, and He clothed them."
>
> Genesis 3:21

There is tenderness in that moment. Despite all the harm they caused, God knew how uncomfortable they had become with their physicality and so He made them clothing and dressed them.

Those were special clothes, very special. The Hebrew word for skin—as in "garments of skin"—is *ohr*. And it just so happens that the word *ohr* is a homonym. *Ohr* also means light and "light."

When God dressed them in *ohr*, He was comforting them. He was telling them that despite the fact that they had failed to reveal the "light," still, all was not lost. The day would yet come when the "light" would finally be revealed. And at that time, just as Moses became a radiant light, mankind would realize its potential, embrace and bask in its relationship with God, and be clothed in *ohr*—in the hidden "light," revealed at last.

> "A new light will shine on Zion. May we all soon merit to benefit from this light."
>
> Daily prayerbook

> "The light that will shine on Zion is none other than the hidden light of creation."
>
> Yavetz, commentary to the prayerbook

NOTES

i. Roberts, J.M. 1993. *History of the World*. New York: Oxford University Press.

ii. Johnson, Paul. 1987. *A History of the Jews*. New York: Harper & Row.

1. Cheilik, Michael. 1991. *Ancient History*. 2nd ed. New York: HarperCollins Publishers.

2. ibid.

3. Roberts, J.M. 1993. *History of the World*. New York: Oxford University Press.

4. Durant, Will. 1963. *Our Oriental Heritage*. New York: Simon and Schuster.

5. Cahill, Thomas. 1998. *The Gifts of the Jews*. New York: Nan A. Talese.

6. Twerski, Abraham J. 1987. *Let Us Make Man*. New York: Traditional Press, Inc.

7. Wilson, Edward O. 1982. *On Human Nature*. Cambridge: Bantam Books.

8. Watson, J.B. 1958. *Behaviorism*. Chicago: University of Chicago Press.

9. Sartre, Jean-Paul. 1969. *Nausea*. New York: New Directions.

10. Luzzato, Moshe C. 1990. *Path of the Just*. Jerusalem: Feldheim.

11. Psalms

12. Boorstin, Daniel J. 1999. *The Seekers*. New York: Vintage Books.

13. Thuan, Trinh Xuan. 2001. *Chaos and Harmony*. New York: Oxford University Press.

14. Weinberg, Steven. *Nature*. Vol. 303. December, 1987.

15. Weinberg, Steven. 1994. *Dreams of a Final Theory*. New York: Vintage Books.

16. Gergen, David. *U.S. News and World Report*. December 12, 1996.

17. National Public Radio. October 13, 1999.

18. Peay, Pythia. *Boundary*. March, 1998.

19. Schlumpf, Heidi. *Publishers Weekly*. August 30, 1999.

20. Poniewozik, James. *Fortune*. September 28, 1998.

21. Lucas, George. *Time*. April 26, 1999.

22. Cahill, Thomas. 1998. *The Gifts of the Jews*. New York: Nan A. Talese.

23. Zeldin, Theodore. 1994. *An Intimate History of Humanity*. New York: HarperCollins Publishers.

24. Roberts, J.M. 1993. *History of the World*. New York: Oxford University Press.

25. Van Doren, Charles. 1991. *A History of Knowledge*. New York: Ballantine Books.

26. Boorstin, Daniel J. 1985. *The Discoverers*. New York: Vintage Books.

27. Van Doren, Charles. 1991. *A History of Knowledge*. New York: Ballantine Books.

ABOUT THE AUTHOR

Shimon Apisdorf is an award-winning author whose books have been read by hundreds of thousands of people around the world. He has gained a world-wide reputation for his ability to extract the essence of classical Jewish wisdom and show how it can be relevant to issues facing the mind, heart and soul in today's world. Shimon grew up in Cleveland, Ohio, and studied at the University of Cincinnati, Telshe Yeshiva of Cleveland and the Aish HaTorah College of Jewish Studies in Jerusalem. He currently resides with his wife, Miriam, and their children in Baltimore. The Apisdorfs enjoy taking long walks, listening to the music of Sam Glaser and going to Orioles games.

Shimon can be reached at sjapisdorf@earthlink.net

Enjoyed Judaism in a Nutshell?

Other books by Shimon Apisdorf are available at better booksellers or by calling 1-800-LEVIATHAN (538-4284). You can also order online at www.leviathanpress.com

ROSH HASHANAH YOM KIPPUR SURVIVAL KIT
by Shimon Apisdorf   1993 Benjamin Franklin Award

PASSOVER SURVIVAL KIT   SURVIVAL KIT FAMILY HAGGADAH
by Shimon Apisdorf   by Shimon Apisdorf

CHANUKAH: *EIGHT NIGHTS OF LIGHT, EIGHT GIFTS FOR THE SOUL*
by Shimon Apisdorf   1997 Benjamin Franklin Award

DEATH OF CUPID   ONE HOUR PURIM PRIMER
by Nachum Braverman   by Shimon Apisdorf
and Shimon Apisdorf

THE BIBLE FOR THE CLUELESS BUT CURIOUS
by Nachum Braverman 1997 Benjamin Franklin Award

MISSILES MASKS AND MIRACLES   REMEMBER MY SOUL
by Charles Samuel   by Lori Palatnik